The Fully Alive Preacher

The Fully Alive Preacher

Recovering from Homiletical Burnout

MIKE GRAVES

Westminster John Knox Press
LOUISVILLE • LONDON

© 2006 Mike Graves
Foreword © 2006 Westminster John Knox Press

Scripture quotations from the New Revised Standard Version of the Bible are copyright © 1989 by the Division of Christian Education of the National Council of the Churches of Christ in the U.S.A. and are used by permission.

Cartoon by Steve Phelps is © Steve Phelps and used by permission.
Cartoons by Doug Hall are © Doug Hall and used by permission.
Sketches of Möbius strip and Picasso's *Bull's Head* are © Rob Quinn and used by permission.
Cartoon by Rob Portlock is © Rob Portlock and used by permission.
Cartoons by Dan Pegoda are © 2005 Dan Pegoda and used by permission.
Cartoon by Ed Koehler is © 2004 Ed Koehler and used by permission.

Book design by Drew Stevens
Cover design by Pam Poll Graphic Design

First edition
Published by Westminster John Knox Press
Louisville, Kentucky

This book is printed on acid-free paper that meets the American National Standards Institute Z39.48 standard. ♾

PRINTED IN THE UNITED STATES OF AMERICA

06 07 08 09 10 11 12 13 14 15—10 9 8 7 6 5 4 3 2 1

Library of Congress Cataloging-in-Publication Data is on file at the Library of Congress, Washington, D.C.

ISBN-13: 978-0-664-23020-3
ISBN-10: 0-664-23020-2

For

Fred Craddock, Tom Long, and Gene Lowry
the homiletical triumvirate who helped renew my preaching

and

Lynn Horak and David May
best friends who help renew my life

CONTENTS

Acknowledgments   ix
Foreword by Barbara Brown Taylor   xiii

Introductory Matters

1. **An Invitation to the Reader**   3
2. **Creating and Re-creating**   15
       The Thrill Is Gone!   15
       A Balancing Act?   19
       A Different Way of Being in the World   22
       Active Spirituality   26
          Renewal: The Sacrament of Looking   29

The Four Stages of Preaching

3. **Stage One: Studying the Scriptures**   35
       Do It Again? Already?   35
       "P" Is *Not* for Procrastination!   38
       Fred Craddock's Two Chairs   41
          Renewal: The Sacrament of Walking   44
       Giving Sermons the Time of Day   46
       Poet or Scholar?   47
       The Devil in the Details?   49
       A Balanced Diet of Sources   52
          Renewal: The Sacrament of Napping   55
       Two Roads Diverged   57
       How Long, O Lord?   59
       Adjusting the Focus   62
       Pet Peeves—Who, Me?   64

4. **Stage Two: Brainstorming Stories**   67
       The Gospel and Groucho   68
       Getting Personal   70
       Painting with a Larger Palette   73
       Stocking the Well   76
          Renewal: The Sacrament of Reading   79
       A Hundred Million Miracles   83

Being Kind to Gremlins 85
Focus, Not Hocus-pocus 87
Orality and Community 89
    Renewal: The Sacrament of Friends 91

5. Stage Three: Creating a Sequence **93**
The Study Becomes Studio 94
Preaching outside the Box 97
Putting a Puzzle Together 101
    Renewal: The Sacrament of Playing 104
Turning the Sermon Upside Down 106
The Plot Thickens 111
A Homiletical Slide Show 115
Drawing a Map 117
Playing with the Pieces 120
    Renewal: The Sacrament of Music 124

6. Stage Four: Embodying the Sermon **127**
The Sermon Becomes Flesh 127
The Sacred but Scary Truth 130
Hide Me behind Something 133
    Renewal: The Sacrament of Movement 135
The Center of Attention 136
Best Supporting Actress 138
To Write or Not to Write? 140
Walking on Water 143
How to Walk on Water 145
    Renewal: The Sacrament of Bread and Wine 150
Presence vs. Precision 151
The Middle Ground 153
More than Mechanics 155
    Renewal: The Sacrament of Dessert 157

Concluding Matters

7. Preaching with Joy 161

Notes 165

ACKNOWLEDGMENTS

Writer David Lynch begins one of his collections of essays with these words: "People sometimes ask me why I write. Because, I tell them, I don't golf." I think I would have to say, "I'm able to write because I also golf." I honestly don't think I could write anything—book, articles, and especially sermons—if it weren't for the outlet golf affords. I am thankful that a sabbatical has allowed me ample time for writing as well as golf, and I hope as you read it will become clear why I say that.

In the writing of books, as in our preaching ministries, we wouldn't make it without the help of others. So let me begin this long list of thank-yous with my family. My wife, Carol, is a wonderful woman whose love is unending and who supported this project in many ways, not the least of which was "holding down the fort" while I was gone for extended periods during my sabbatical leave. Thanks also to our children—Michael, Melissa, and Michelle. Your love enriches my life.

Professionally, I'm grateful to my colleagues at Central Baptist Theological Seminary—the faculty, administration, and the board—for graciously allowing me this sabbatical leave. To my ears, *sabbatical* has to be one of the most beautiful words in the English language.

I also wish to thank the Continuing Education staff of Princeton Theological Seminary, who allowed me to field-test this material on two separate occasions. Thanks especially to David H. Wall, Joyce C. Tucker, Susan Repko, and my good friend on the homiletical faculty there, Cleo LaRue Jr. Moreover, I'm grateful to the ministers who gathered there at Princeton to listen to my ideas and share theirs with me.

I'm also grateful to the kind people with the Church of Scotland for inviting me to give the 2005 Warrack Lectures as I was putting the finishing touches on this book: Nigel Robb for extending the invitation and several of the persons who hosted me in various ways—John Chalmers, Gavin Elliott, Jane Denniston, Dorothy Davidson, and Moira Whyte. A special thanks to Alan and Judith McDonald in Saint Andrews, whose Scottish hospitality was warm indeed. Thanks for the good food and for the golf on such sacred sites!

I am also indebted to the staff of the Cathedral College (formerly the College of Preachers) under the auspices of the National Cathedral in Washington, D.C., who appointed me a Fellow there in the fall of 2004. What a gift, to study and write in that rich environment! Thanks to Howard Anderson, Dean McDonald, Shelagh Casey Brown, Kim Gilliam, Joan Roberts, and Alice S. Morrow Rowan of the college, as well as the gifted chefs, Charlie Dunne and Hassent Lunzel. The fried chicken was to die for! I am also grateful for the opportunity to spend time with my "fellow Fellow" that fall, Laurie Hays Coffman, who is one of God's good gifts to this world and who on more than one occasion listened to me babble about this project.

My conversations with parish ministers—some of whom I wish to thank by name—has greatly enriched my thinking. This book would not exist if it weren't for Jim Gordon—at least not in its present form. I am grateful beyond words for his impact on this project and my life. Besides Jim, others offered inspiration and reflection: Robert Fugarino, who is always full of good ideas; Marcus McFaul, who offered constant encouragement; and Carol Wade, with whom I broke bread (quesadillas really) and talked preaching. You are all amazing!

I am also deeply indebted to fellow homiletician David Schlafer, who offered counsel beyond the call of duty during my stay in D.C., and his wife, Peggy, who both so graciously hosted me while away from my family. The salmon and red snapper were superb, and give my regards to your poodle, Brigita. David is a part of the Academy of Homiletics, that wonderful group of scholars who nourish my soul through their books, but even more so through their lives at our annual meetings.

Thanks also to the kind people at FedEx for permission to use their logo, especially Cortney Cannon, who offered a friendly voice to go along with their corporate identity. Rob Quinn's artistic talents have always blessed my life, and in this volume he has also offered assistance with some sketches. Thanks as well to Steve Phelps, Ed Koehler, Dan Pegoda, Rob Portlock, and Doug Hall, all of them gifted cartoonists who gave permission to use their copyrighted works. Your humor has enriched these pages. Lastly, I am grateful for the editorial work of Stephanie Egnotovich, who helped give birth to this sabbatical work. This book is better because of you and your gifts.

Sabbatical truly is one of the most beautiful words in the English language — that and *golf*. I don't know if I've ever lived a richer six months. Thanks be to God!

FOREWORD

If you have picked up this book, then either you are a preacher who is a little singed around the edges, or else you know someone who is. Either way, you have come to the right place. There is no flogging in these pages, no overly cheerful coaching of the preacher to buck up and get back on purpose. Instead, there is the tantalizing invitation to discover a purpose deeper than producing serviceable sermons on a weekly basis, by deciding to become a deeper human being.

Mike Graves has preached long enough to know how the steady exposure of the pulpit can sunburn the spirit. He has taught preachers long enough to know how the manifold responsibilities of ministry can dull the soul. On both counts, he knows better than to complain about these occupational hazards of the preaching life. They go with the territory, and the only way to avoid them is to stay in bed on Sunday mornings. His good news for those who wish to keep preaching is that the cure for what ails us is not more skills, more workshops, or more books, but *more life*—and especially the simple pleasures of life that preachers routinely forgo.

While this book includes four valuable sections on sermon preparation, it also features compelling invitations to walk, to nap, to read, to play, and to eat dessert. In Graves's vision, these are not spoons full of sugar to make the medicine go down but forms of "active spirituality" that keep preachers connected to the springs of God's good gifts in this life. Without them, the sound that sermons make can easily become the sound of empty buckets scraping dry sand.

Graves also tells stories that trigger bodily recognition of the truths he tells, and asks questions that beg to be answered. What are your Saturdays like? Where do you sit to prepare your sermons? What strikes you most about your body as a vehicle for the gospel? How does it feel to call yourself a preacher? Sensing how deep some of these questions may go, he adds silly cartoons, suggested exercises, and scriptural passages for meditation, all of which result in a book that reads more like a conversation with an old friend than like a text by a professor of preaching. For this reason, those who finish it quickly may wish that they had read more slowly—or they may look forward to reading it again.

While Graves has written this book for burned-out preachers, there is wisdom here for burned-out Christians as well—indeed, for anyone living too busy a life in too busy a world. Wherever service has extinguished pleasure and earnestness has replaced joy, there is urgent need for the sacraments of renewal that Mike Graves celebrates in this text.

The glory of God is a human being fully alive, wrote the Christian sage Irenaeus almost two thousand years ago. You who have picked up this book are now in the best position to decide whether or not he was right and—if he was—to glorify God through your own aliveness, by embodying the gospel as you alone can.

BARBARA BROWN TAYLOR

Clarkesville, Georgia
All Saints' Day 2005

Introductory Matters

ONE

AN INVITATION
TO THE READER

If preaching is intended to enliven the church, why is it killing so many ministers?

I mean *killing* figuratively, of course. Or maybe not. As Brother David Steindl-Rast writes, "That you have not yet died is not sufficient proof that you're alive."[1] Still, the question haunts me: If preaching is intended to enliven the church, why is it killing so many ministers? For some time now that question has been foremost on my mind. But judging from the preachers I've talked to, it describes a deeply felt anxiety shared by many.

This is a book for preachers who've been at their calling long enough that they have not only considerable experience, but possibly a case of burnout as well. Not ministerial burnout in general, which is a common subject of books these days, but rather a more specific malady, homiletical burnout. I'm thinking of ministers who know what it means to dread yet another sermon, yet another Sunday. Maybe it's the overall drudgery of preaching, or perhaps it's the toll of revealing ourselves in public week after week. Homiletical burnout. The question is what to do about it.

Most of the preaching books written these days focus on other aspects of preaching—usually one of two issues.[2] A few books, very few, call for the church to rethink its theology of preaching, suggesting that the problem with preaching these days lies with the thinking that undergirds what we do on Sundays.[3] What welcome news! Preaching is a theological act, no doubt about it, and because it is the bedrock of our proclamation, for some ministers a renewed appreciation of the homiletical task and its theological nuances could renew their perspective.

More common is the second type of book, the book designed to cultivate a set of skills. True, attention to sharpening skills can often reinvigorate a minister's preaching. In part, that explains why so many ministers attend preaching workshops and retreats. They are looking to hone their skills.

Seminaries model this same dual approach to teaching preaching—theory and practice—with the proportions varying from one institution to the next. So there is the theology of preaching and the practice of preaching. It's a workable system, up to a point.

But once a person has learned how to think about preaching and has done it long enough to become relatively proficient, what is most wrong might be something else entirely: Soul, or, more precisely, what William Wordsworth labeled dullness of soul.[4] Now by *soul*, I don't mean some Greek philosophical soul or the kind that raving street preachers want to save. No, I mean something else entirely. I mean *soul* as in *soul food*, the kind of vittles intended to fill more than your belly. I mean *soul* as in how someone might describe a quaint used bookstore as the "heart and *soul*" of a neighborhood. I mean *soul* the way Harry Emerson Fosdick used it in his hymn "God of Grace and God of Glory," the line about how we can be "rich in things and poor in *soul*." By *soul* I mean the very lifeblood of the preacher.

Irenaeus, the early church theologian, put it this way: The glory of God is a human being fully alive. How many preachers these days can be described as fully alive? How many of us would describe ourselves in that way? The grammatically inventive poet e. e. cummings put it this way: "Life, for most people, simply isn't."[5] What's wrong with preaching these days may be more a matter of what's wrong with us preachers.

Anne Lamott, reflecting on writer's block, has captured the problem best in a statement that will not let me go: "If your wife locks you out of the house, you don't have a problem with your door." Such a brilliant observation! She continues, "The word *block* suggests that you are constipated or stuck, when the truth is that you are empty."[6] That's it. Too many preachers would have to admit to being empty. Sound familiar?

In this book my primary interest is how our approach to preaching—and life—allows room for God to renew us—or doesn't. We preach, for instance, about forgiveness and grace but often carry around a load of guilt related to the lack of time we spent preparing for Sunday's sermon. Or we preach about joy but have long since lost our zeal for the task of proclamation. We preach about thanksgiving no longer grateful to be preaching at all—or at least not very often. As Karl Barth observed, "If it were toilsome and dull for ministers to do their Sunday work, how could they expect the congregation and the world to find it refreshing?"[7] Parker Palmer refers to this disconnect as a violation of "role and soul," a draining tension between who we are and what we do.[8]

Imagine a woman who owns a small restaurant. She prepares the meals, yes, but she also keeps the books, trains new help, makes sure the facilities are in line with the city's sanitation codes, deals with happy as well as disgruntled customers, pays the bills, orders supplies—the list goes on and on. It's enough to deter anyone from opening a restaurant. Unless! Unless you take great delight in feeding people! What if she opened the restaurant in the first place simply because she wanted to feed people? What if she believed then, and probably still does down deep somewhere, that feeding people is a gracious act of hospitality? Over time, however, what started out as calling and mission and great fun has become drudgery. Days go by when she never thinks of how feeding folks is a holy undertaking.

Do you know any preachers like that, people who have a calling to feed God's flock through the preached word, but for whom the whole enterprise has become just that—an enterprise—when it used to be a sacred privilege? Maybe that describes your own state of mind these days.

Thus, in this book I extend two invitations to readers. The first is an invitation to reflect on your own relationship with preaching—the joys, the anxieties, the frustrations, the tedium, the moments of ecstasy as well as agony, the reasons you became a preacher in the first place. This first invitation is a personal one that can best be appreciated in light of two stories.

A few years ago at the annual meeting of the Academy of

Homiletics, Joseph (Joey) Jeter, who teaches preaching at Brite Divinity School in Fort Worth, Texas, preached one evening. Wouldn't you know it, what I remember best is a story he shared with us about a former student. She had taken a preaching course with him because it was required. Period. She wasn't the least bit interested in preaching. Chaplaincy maybe, but she most definitely didn't consider herself a preacher. But as often happens in seminaries everywhere—and it seems, more often with female students than male—she discovered she really was created to be a preacher. She fell in love with preaching, and after graduating became the pastor of a church in a small Texas town, where she gave herself to the people and the weekly task of preaching.

Then tragedy. One day, a garbage truck ran a red light and broadsided her car, pinning her inside. Rescue crews used those large mechanical jaws to pry her out of what was left of her automobile. Two miracles: one, she was alive, and two, no brain damage. When she regained consciousness at the hospital, the doctor told her of the extensive surgeries that would be needed. Just before she drifted off to sleep, she smiled and said four words, "I can still preach!"

That is the kind of story a preacher remembers. In fact, a year or so later I was leading a workshop on preaching; as I concluded the session, I decided to "throw that story in" at the end. I hadn't planned to do so, but it seemed right. How was I to know the impact that it would have on one of the preachers there and, as a result, on my life too?

That preacher was Jim Gordon, pastor of Pine Ridge Presbyterian Church in Kansas City, Missouri, a couple of miles from where I live. I had met Jim prior to that workshop, but didn't know him well. He e-mailed me a few days after that session to say how much that story had meant to him, and asked if we could get together for lunch. Over a meal, Jim told me about a stroke he had suffered years earlier, when he was only in his thirties, and how at the time it wasn't certain he would be able to preach again, or even to speak, for that matter. Jim has recovered fully from the incident, thanks be to God, and so understandably the story of that Texas pastor and her four words, "I can still preach," touched him in deep places.

Since that first lunch, Jim and I have eaten lots of meals

together. We've read lots of books together, novels and the like, but mostly books on preaching. We talk preaching on the phone some, as well as personal stuff, running into each other at our daughters' dance recitals. We e-mail each other on occasion with homiletical questions. I've worshiped at his church many times and have always enjoyed his preaching, as well as the times I've preached there. But without question our richest professional exchanges are those times when we get together to eat and to talk about preaching. That is the first invitation, to get together—as author and reader—to reflect on your approach to preaching.

When Jim and I get together though, the topic is often bigger than preaching. We talk about our lives—books we've read, movies we've seen, our kids' birthday parties, the best fish and chips in Kansas City. In short, life. This is where the second invitation comes in, an invitation to reconsider your approach to life in general, specifically how the preaching life is more holistic than some ministers might imagine. The second invitation is an invitation to rethink your approach to life's little pleasures.

For some of us a life is what we had before seminary and ministry. Wesley Allen, who teaches at Lexington Theological Seminary, tells a story about one of his own seminary professors, Brevard Childs, the renowned Old Testament scholar. In class one day a student asked him what it would take to get an A on an exegesis paper. Childs responded, "If you want to do better exegesis, become a deeper person."[9] What wisdom! The same goes for the homiletical task. If we want to be better preachers, we should first consider how we might become deeper persons. Or to put it in the vernacular, if we want to get up sermons for the next umpteen years, we had better get a life first!

The two invitations—to rethink our approach to preaching and our approach to life—are related, to be sure, but each also demands a closer look. So let's consider them in more detail.

Our Approach to Preaching

I have arranged our discussion of preaching under four general headings, each a stage of sermon preparation: studying the Scriptures, brainstorming stories, creating a sequence, and embodying the sermon. These stages span the preaching task from the very beginning of the process to the moment of proclamation on Sunday morning. The first, *studying the Scriptures*, is about our stewardship of the textual and theological issues involved in preaching. We begin as stewards of the Word. The second, *brainstorming stories*, reminds us that sermons must deal with the modern world as well as the text, making connections. The third stage, *creating a sequence*, is where we decide how these two worlds will come together on Sunday, the sermon's flow or structure. The final stage, *embodying the sermon*, is the moment of truth, when we stand before a congregation with what we hope is a relevant and engaging word from God.

Of the roughly four million (give or take a million) aspects of sermon preparation preachers consider each week, I have highlighted four key stages. If only one of these stages suffers, the results can be disastrous. Imagine, for instance, a sermon that is anything but boring; it's well crafted and presented dramatically, except that noticeably absent is any kind of serious theological reflection or biblical substance. The sermon is interesting but a lot like cotton candy—not much there to bite into.

Or perhaps the exegesis is admirable, the focus of the message clear enough, the preacher's presence dynamic, but, alas, there are no stories. Never once a sentence that begins, "Did you see in the news the other day about that woman who . . ." or "I remember in college a bunch of my friends had . . ." A sermon without stories can be deadly. In a word, boring!

Or maybe the sermon contains all the right sources—quotes by Walter Brueggemann; all the right stories—maybe one by Garrison Keillor, from out on the edge of the prairie; all the presence listeners could ask for—Meryl Streep in the pulpit; but it is very hard to follow. The sequence or flow just doesn't work, and people drive home from church scratching their heads and wondering, "What was that all about?"

Or maybe the preacher's study, stories, and sequencing are just fine, but the sermon is read from a manuscript in a monotone voice. I know several people whose ministers do just that. Their response? "I can stay home and *read* a sermon, thank you very much!" Clearly, embodying the sermon is important.

Reflection in all four of these stages of sermon preparation is crucial, looking at the big picture. But more than that, personal reflection is needed. Does the way you go about the preaching task within each of these four stages work for you? It is a pressing question for many ministers. Unfortunately, overwhelmed with concerns of preparing *this week's sermon*, we rarely have time to consider the overall process we use week after week. Imagine a high school student who struggles in an advanced course, physics, for instance. She doesn't understand the assignments. Every night she complains about the difficulty of the homework. Her parents keep suggesting a tutor, but all she can think of is finishing tomorrow's homework. Caught up in the day-to-day grind, she finds it hard to step back and look at the big picture. As a result, she never really comprehends the subject.

When we reflect on the larger scope of our preaching ministries, that big picture can provide perspective and renewal. For instance, it is fairly common for ministers to preach various kinds of sermons — different approaches to sequence, such as narrative or inductive, instead of the traditional three points — if for no other reason than to maintain sanity in the midst of routine. Ministers who don't try different forms often fall into a homiletical rut from which they can't get up. But the shape of our sermons, which relates to what I call creating a sequence, is only one aspect of our preaching. What about the actual preaching of the sermon — stage four? What about our use of notes, for instance? What about our approach to study? What about the rhythm of our weekly routine? You get the idea.

At each stage in the book we will reflect on one overriding concern, Is your approach to preaching self-renewing or not? This is a far different issue from whether your approach works, though they are not mutually exclusive. I'm interested not only in whether your approach works — which might justify your routine or the occasional rut — but also if it fits you.

Richard Lischer, in his Lyman Beecher Lectures on preaching, rightly notes that we can become too preoccupied with finding our own style, neglecting the style that the text itself calls for.[10] Balance, of course, is the key, because we can also deny our personal style, never find our own way. Thus, some key questions we will wrestle with: Does the way you preach enliven you, or wear you down? Have you discovered your own unique approach to preaching, or do you feel more as if you're a kid wearing one of you dad's T-shirts? Does the way you were taught to preach fit you, or do you feel like a left-handed child forced to use your right hand? (I speak here from experience.) Where homiletical burnout exists, it may be more a matter of rethinking our *approach* to the preaching task than the task itself.

Within each of the four stages of sermon preparation the topics discussed are offered in bite-size pieces, one to three pages or so, entries you could read in one brief sitting. Because each entry concludes with questions for reflection, you might think of the book as a journal, with plenty of space for jotting down your thoughts. You may decide to work through the questions alone, or with colleagues in a ministerial alliance or a book group. Or a conversation over a meal might be just the thing.

Each entry also concludes with a verse of Scripture for reflection. The biblical references are brief, very brief. Normally, you'd look them up in their context and exegete them. That's what ministers do. Resist the urge in this case. These snippets of Scripture are offered in the spirit of divine reading (*lectio divina*), in which you are invited to read slowly and closely. With this approach to reading, the idea is not to make it through the whole Bible in a year but rather to let the words of Scripture make their way into your heart, no matter how long that takes. The space below each reading will, I hope, allow you to take an unhurried approach, allowing room for God's Spirit to speak to yours.

Our Approach to Life

Most of us are familiar with the classic monastic practices that Thomas Merton and more recently Richard Foster have made popular, even though they are as old as religion—fasting, contemplative prayer, and meditation.[11] For many of us, these practices ground us spiritually, but perhaps these practices do not capture the whole of our existence. What of life's simple pleasures?

Even in Christianity's infancy, believers struggled with how to relate to this world and its pleasures. Proponents of gnosticism and docetism insisted that physical matter was inferior to spiritual things, that even Christ had not been really human. It was in just such a context that Irenaeus penned his now famous words, about God's glory being made manifest in persons who are "fully alive." Fully alive to God. Fully alive to God's good creation.[12]

Perhaps you recall that scene in C. S. Lewis's *The Screwtape Letters* when the elder devil Screwtape warns his understudy Wormwood against letting humans enjoy life's simple pleasures. Scathingly, he chides:

> On your own showing you first of all allowed the patient to read a book he really enjoyed, because he enjoyed it and not in order to make clever remarks about it to his new friends. In the second place, you allowed him to walk down to the old mill and have tea there—a walk through country he really likes, and taken alone. In other words you allowed him two real positive Pleasures. Were you so ignorant as not to see the danger of this? . . .
>
> I would make it a rule to eradicate from my patient any strong personal taste which is not actually a sin, even if it is something quite trivial such as a fondness for country cricket or collecting stamps or drinking cocoa.[13]

What are those moments in addition to times of prayer and Scripture reading when you are most alive? When you are not attending a meeting of some sort, what helps you to feel most alive, most appreciative of God's good gifts in this world? Maybe it's one of these:

Gardening	Antique restoration	Golf
Hiking	Cross-country skiing	Quilting
Fresh raspberries	Playing guitar	Tennis
Kite flying	Poetry	Jogging
A good book	Pizza	Making candles
Drawing	Softball	Making love
Bird watching	Family reunion	Throwing horseshoes
Ice cream	Short stories	Playing catch

The list goes on and on, of course, but I suspect one or more of these resonates with you and/or reminds you of another form of active spirituality. Perhaps the printed word alone on the page is enough to trigger memories of renewal.

Nancy Malone, in her book on the spirituality of reading, describes such a moment in her own life:

I walk down to the beach this early October afternoon to see if the tide is right for a swim. Two swans, accustomed to being fed there, come waddling toward me on their splayed feet. I hold out my hands to show them I have no food. They stop, fold their legs beneath themselves, and tuck their orange beaks under their wings, perfectly symmetrical. On the weather-worn raft beached by the outgoing tide (too low for swimming), a cormorant holds its gray-black serrated wings stretched at full span, unmoving against the blue sky. I lie down, a piece of driftwood under my head, and feel the warmth of the sand through my jeans and shirt. Out of the breeze the sun is hot. What am I doing? Nothing. Enjoying the sun, gazing at the white swans, the black cormorant, the tranquil bay, the wide sky.[14]

Whether we recognize it or not, this is a form of *spiritual* renewal. "What am I doing?" she asks. "Nothing." Or maybe *Everything*! Made in the image of God, and part of God's creation, we are truly renewed by such moments in life. As Paul Tillich is supposed to have claimed, "The whole earth is God's monastery." When we deny ourselves life's good pleasures, Julia Cameron observes, we become like a divorced person who is way too curious about our ex's love life, miserable and envious.[15]

The idea of ministers actually enjoying life is a foreign concept for some. Influenced perhaps by one particular model of atonement theory—that one must suffer on behalf of the many—some ministers believe it their lot in life to be miserable, to give of themselves until there is nothing left to give. But that is only one model of atonement and only one approach to ministry in general. Suffering *with* those whom we serve is quantitatively different than suffering *in their stead*. And what of our congregation's joys in life? What of our own lives?

I remember the moment when, early in my ministry, I learned that life could be enjoyed. The insight came from a book, not a scholarly work per se, but a good book nonetheless—Tim Hansel's *When I Relax, I Feel Guilty*. As I think back on my reading of that book, I recall a sunny day, sitting in my car and waiting for my wife to get off work. I remember a sense of euphoria, a kind of primal giggling down deep in my soul.

The revelation? That I could be in the world in a different sort of way, even enjoy life.

And what does all of this say about our preaching? More than we might first imagine. In his classic homiletics text *The Ministry of the Word*, R. E. C. Browne compares the making of a sermon to the making of bread, drawing all sorts of wonderful parallels.[16] I want to suggest, however, that actually baking bread—mixing flour, water, salt, and yeast together, kneading dough, sticking it in the oven, eating it hot while the butter melts—is a sermonic act of sorts. Not literally of course, but renewing nonetheless, since as preachers we are—believe it or not—people. People, for whom the act of baking and eating homemade bread is renewing. When we are renewed as persons, we are renewed as preachers.

Because a walk on the beach and eating homemade bread can renew us as persons, I also include pieces of renewal woven throughout the book. I call these entries *sacraments of renewal*, and I do not use the term *sacraments* lightly. I intend it in the sense that these are God's good gifts to us, means of embodying grace in our lives, taking grace into our bodies. I've included ten sacraments in all: looking, walking, napping, reading, friends, playing, music, movement, bread and wine, and, last but not least, dessert. No doubt, you will think of others.

If the four homiletical stages serve as the book's spine, the sacraments of renewal are its nervous system. These ten pieces are sprinkled throughout, sometimes in logical places but sometimes unexpectedly, much like life's pleasures. Rather than concluding these sacramental pieces with reflection questions, however, I offer suggestions for "preacher dates," an idea I have borrowed from Julia Cameron, whose creative work has influenced my life and this book in many ways. "Preacher dates" are time away for yourself, ways to indulge your creative self. The date doesn't have to be long; it's quality time we're after, not necessarily great quantities of time. Cameron advises, "Spending time in solitude with your artist child is essential to self-nurturing. A long country walk, a solitary expedition to the beach for a sunrise or sunset, a sortie out to a strange church to hear gospel music, to an ethnic neighborhood to taste foreign sights and sounds—your artist might enjoy any of these. Or your artist might like bowling."[17] Reread that last sentence substituting the word *preacher* for *artist* and you'll get the idea. If the concept of preacher dates seems childish, trust me, you'll get over it. Besides, recall Jesus' words about becoming as little children. Or as Pablo Picasso put it, "When I was four, I could draw as well as Raphael. It has taken me my whole life to learn to draw like a four-year-old child."

TWO

CREATING AND RE-CREATING

"Brother Helvey is here with the black box from last night's sermon to see if we can find out what went wrong."

The Thrill Is Gone!

We begin with a parable, from a 1998 broadcast of National Public Radio's *This American Life*. On this particular episode they honored Valentine's Day with stories of love, but not the typical romantic variety. The tale I'm referring to was a quirky little story about a couple, Richard and Linda, who'd been married for more than nine years, with two kids, and careers. One day the family went for a frozen yogurt treat, and Linda recognized a man in the store, a former boyfriend who looked better than ever. His name was David, and he was a psychologist like herself. The attraction between them was clear; Linda, this old flame David, even the husband Richard could tell. The attraction was that obvious.

Linda and David engaged in some small talk with just a hint of flirting beneath the surface. Then Linda and her family left. But this chance encounter was all she could think of—this gorgeous man and the feeling that had come over her in the yogurt store. When she got to work on Monday, she had a voice mail from David. She ignored it, but he called again, definitely flirting. She knew better, but then thought it couldn't hurt just to return his call. David suggested they get together for coffee and conversation some time.

Maybe it was the fact she's a psychologist—who knows—but Linda decided to ask her husband Richard what he thought. He admitted he wasn't too thrilled, but he trusted her. "Whatever you think," he said. Linda told her husband she could hardly stop thinking about David, that she was obsessed, even fantasizing about this man from her past.

Then, in a moment of brilliance and tenderness, Richard put his arms around his wife and said, "Honey, I'm so sorry I can't do that for you anymore." That was all. No speeches. No scolding. Just, "Honey, I'm so sorry I can't do that for you anymore." Linda picked up the phone immediately and called David. She told him what had just happened, including what her husband had said. She told David what a wonderful man she was married to and told him never to call her again. She realized what she had right there. "Honey, I'm so sorry I can't do that for you anymore."

In a day when so many marriages end with one spouse or another looking for greener grass, Linda and Richard's story is truly inspiring. There is something grand to be said for faithfulness even when the thrill is long gone. Plugging along, doing the best you can even when you don't feel like it. End of parable.

Parables, of course, entail laying one thing next to another. We preachers, too, should be commended for plugging along Sunday after Sunday for years, doing the best we can even when we don't feel like it. The thrill is gone, but still we prepare. Still we plod along. Oh, sure there are rare weeks when some of the thrill is back, but they are rare; yet we keep preparing. Do we have a choice?

Still, I can't help but wonder who among us wouldn't suggest that in addition to commending such faithfulness, maybe some counsel is in order, encouragement to put some sizzle back in the romance. We're talking about preaching, I remind you, and as Henry David Thoreau so aptly reminds us, "You must get your living by loving."[1] Whether we like to admit it or not, some of us are in need of serious homiletical counseling.

It may be hard to remember, but we used to be excited at the prospects of preaching a real sermon during a real worship service. Not that devotional some friend asked us to give before the youth group departed for a mission trip one sleepy Monday morning. No, a real Sunday morning sermon.

My first preaching opportunity came in the summer of 1979, a couple of years before I began seminary. I was serving a church as ministerial intern, a program that had been created for college students who were seminary bound. In addition to attending the weekly staff meeting and being part of a bus ministry for children who would not be able to attend church otherwise, we tagged along with the "real ministers" on hospital visits and the like. On one such visit, the person in the next bed was a pastor, who when he discovered we were ministers told us he probably wouldn't be out by the weekend. He confided that he wasn't sure who would preach for him, paused, and then asked me if I would. "I'd be glad to," I said, as if I'd preached hundreds of times. I didn't see any reason to worry the poor man. I spent the next fifty hours—OK, maybe it was sixty hours—getting ready to preach my first sermon. Sure, I was scared, but only the way kids are when looking up at the roller coaster—an excited scariness. I relished that August Sunday and the other opportunities that came my way here and there over the next few years.

We used to be so excited and enthralled with preparing and preaching sermons. Remember? But like a fizzling marriage, along the way something happened. Listen to how Linda Carolyn Loving describes her own relationship (yes, *relationship*) with preaching:

I have a love/hate relationship with preaching. Always have, always will. I hate preaching the most when I go to bed at 9:35 p.m. on a Saturday night, knowing that other "real people" are out seeing newly released movies or flirting over a plate of Pad Thai or having a glass of wine at intermission, and I . . . I, the preacher for the next morning, am crawling into bed pretending that I am content with my sermon and pretending that I will sleep. . . . I love preaching the most when I am singing the closing hymn at the second service and know that in forty-five minutes I will be in my sweats at the Louisiana Café reading the *New York Times* and eating hash browns and letting go. . . . Definitely, a love/hate relationship.[2]

Personal Reflection

What is your favorite part of preaching? How would you describe it? An adventure? A treat? What is your least favorite part? How would you describe it? A drudgery? A bear? A burden? Something not fit to print? Recall your first sermon and early preaching adventures. What stands out in your mind?

Scriptural Meditation

> *"The word is near you, on your lips and in your heart." (Romans 10:8)*

A Balancing Act?

To understand the relationship between our preaching and our lives, we must first consider the traditional way of viewing work and play. No doubt, for most of us the following seesaw will seem very familiar.

Work   **Play**

_____

∧

On one side of the seesaw is work. In the pastorate, work includes things such as *administrative duties* (You can capitalize that one if you wish!), *hospital visits, committee work, sermon preparation, counseling, worship planning*. I'll leave it up to you in what order to write those things; I buried *sermon preparation* in the middle.

On the other side is play. You may have to look that one up. It's in the dictionary, trust me. Under *play* one might suggest *gardening*, another *golf*, still another *baking cookies* or *riding a bike* or *time with family*. Associated with the word *play* are all those things we thoroughly enjoy, even if only on rare occasions of renewal.

The fulcrum is the key in the traditional model. Thus the seesaw can take on different forms. Heavy on work with little or no play. Or vice versa, ministers who, because they are largely held unaccountable for their whereabouts during the week, hardly work at all.

When work and play are viewed in this seesaw manner, the only hope is to seek balance. Most preachers I know struggle to achieve such balance. Their struggle resembles the old Western movies where two cowboys are wrestling on top of a moving train. One of them wears a badge, the other has a mask about his face. The wrestling is fierce! Clearly, one of them is going to lose, be thrown off the train, maybe even die as a result.[3] Who will win? As Parker Palmer points out, most of us live our lives between the two poles of work and play, either by *separation* or *alternation*.[4] With the separation approach we must choose, as we see in the cartoon of the vacationing minister.

If you're in the boat at the theme park, it's not time to be looking for preaching metaphors! Work and play are separate! If

"You're on vacation! Stop looking for metaphors!"

forced to choose between the two, some opt for a laid-back approach to ministry—which in extreme form can result in laziness. Others adopt the world's standards of productivity—which in extreme form can consume us. Truth be told, neither the lazy minister nor the workaholic is a model of wise balance, and in the traditional approach balance is key. You remember those seesaws from when you were a kid. After riding up and down for a while, you and your friend decided to balance one another midair. Not an easy task!

If the choice we make is work over play, a fairly common choice ministers make, then exhaustion inevitably leads us to alternation, what Palmer calls the "vacation approach to life."[5] We've worked hard for fifty weeks; it's time to take off two weeks, even if a sermon will be due when we return. Truth be told, we're a strange lot when it comes to finding value in our work. Dorothy Bass tells about a group of teachers complaining about all the grading they had to do, having promised students to return their papers by Monday. Before long, however, the complaining became one-upmanship. "Someone listening in might have thought we were competing to see who had to grade the most, who worked hardest, and who was most put upon by the demands of his or her job."[6] I think I've heard the ministerial version of that same conversation, haven't you?

Ask any person who's about to go on vacation, minister or otherwise, how life's treating them and the answer is "Great! We leave tomorrow for _____." Ask them a month, or in our case, one Sunday, after returning and the answer is often not fit to print. Alternation is superior to separation, true, but both lend themselves to burnout, that well-known clergy disease for which there seems to be no cure. When we live like this, Julia Cameron observes, we become like circus animals, tigers that can jump through hoops on demands; in a word, "on" when we need to be, but obviously lifeless.[7]

Corporate America knows that their European counterparts are more productive even with—or *because* they have—more weeks off per year, but still we are consumed with work, unable to believe that well-rested workers are the best kind. Productivity reigns supreme with blue collar, white collar, and ministerial collar, alike!

So the minister works on the sermon when not working on some administrative task, when not making a hospital visit, when not dealing with some personality conflict between parishioners, when not . . . and the list goes on and on. And if we're lucky, we actually take off a day every once in a while.

Repeat this for fifty weeks or so, for forty years or better, with a sabbatical thrown in if we're really lucky, then call it a ministry, a life spent for God and church. The result: we are truly spent!

Personal Reflection

Where does sermon preparation fit in your weekly schedule at present? Has that changed over the years? How so? Where do sermon preparation and self-care rank in your priorities, not ideally, but at the end of most weeks? What would you like to change?

Scriptural Meditation

"Those who wait for the LORD shall renew their strength." (*Isaiah 40:31*)

_____

_____

_____

_____

_____

_____

_____

_____

_____

_____

A Different Way of Being in the World

I think about that Norman Rockwell painting where a busy downtown street, probably somewhere in Manhattan, is filled with workers bustling about, briefcases in hand, on their way to the office, no doubt. Nowadays, they'd have a cell phone to their ears as well. To a person, they are looking down at the sidewalk as they hurry to the job that so desperately beckons. Behind them are the large wooden doors of a downtown church, with a minister changing the sign on the marquee. It reads, "Lift Up Thine Eyes."

Sure, Rockwell's paintings all portray — some would say *imagine* — an America of idealism, white picket fences, and time for grace over meals. Still, taking time out of a busy schedule seems a relevant word for a people whose God models Sabbath in the rhythms of the creation story and commands it for our own good. Some of us have nearly killed ourselves while working on sermons about Sabbath. Go figure!

Julia Cameron puts it bluntly when she notes how sometimes "we are too busy living a life to have a life worth living."[8] There is another way besides *separation* and *alternation*, though. Parker Palmer calls it *integration*, in which "contemplation-and-action" are hyphenated, implying "what our language obscures: that the one cannot exist without the other."[9] In this third way we discover how to hold action and contemplation—work and play if you prefer—in proper tension.

Palmer adapts an image for the proper tension of work and play from the nineteenth-century German mathematician and astronomer August Ferdinand Möbius. It's called a Möbius strip. You start with a piece of paper, say eight inches long and one inch wide. If you joined the ends they would form a circle, a bracelet of sorts—only one of the ends is given a half-twist first.

The Möbius strip serves as a vivid reminder that who we are on the inside and what we do on the outside are one. Our personhood and preaching role cannot be separated from each other. Palmer writes, "Whether we know it or not, like it or not, accept it or not, we all live on the Möbius strip all the time."[10]

So the minister is on vacation, and maybe while having fun he comes across a lovely metaphor that will preach. Often, when we are relaxed, that sort of thing happens. Why not write it down? Most of us would respond, "Good idea, jot it down." But what about playing on the job? Say the minister is in her study, and while looking for some report, she comes across a short story someone passed along. Why not read it, right? Many ministers I know would admit to more than a twinge of guilt for reading a short story "on the clock."

But imagine for a moment a different way of living. What if one morning you are working on your sermon, when about 9:30 or so you realize it's time to head for the hospital. A church member is scheduled for surgery, and you of course want to be there to offer support. After a time of prayer and presence, including some time spent waiting with the family, you decide it would be all right to leave now. You drive back another route, maybe even with the windows down and a favorite CD playing. Why? Why not?

En route, you come across a lovely park, or an ice cream store—clearly one of God's great gifts to humanity—or maybe even a park with an ice cream store nearby. So you take a short walk with some cookies-and-cream. You return to the church and look back over notes you hope will give birth to a sermon, as well as returning some calls. You eat lunch with a colleague in ministry. You work on a civic project in the afternoon, perhaps sneak in a game of tennis later that day or "work" in your garden before picking up the kids or running some errands. In the evening you attend a meeting. Late that night you read a short passage from the Psalms before falling asleep. Question: What part of the day has been sermon preparation, and what part has been self-care? Answer: It is all sermon preparation, and it is all self-care. It is all part of life, the only one you have.

If this approach to ministry and life seems too simplistic, then consider the life of C. S. Lewis. Lewis's life as teacher and writer was consistently interrupted by the demands of caring for his adopted mother—housework, shopping, walking the dog, and so forth. Lewis's brother Warnie lamented that Lewis could have been so much more productive if not for all the interruptions, but his biographer, A. N. Wilson, disagrees. And apparently so did Lewis himself. He believed that it was the interruptions to his study time that fostered not only a degree of productivity, but his creativity as well.[11]

When we have known only one way of being in the world, it's hard to imagine another, especially if a new way challenges the long-standing Puritan work ethic pounded into many of us. Or maybe another way threatens us. For instance, when Google, the well-known Internet search engine, was debating going public with stock offerings, one of the biggest internal struggles related to corporate expectations. Google is the kind of workplace where beanbag chairs are favored over cubicles and employees use scooters to get around headquarters. They play beach volleyball and take naps if they want to. In short, they have fun in their work. What if investors insisted on more hard-and-fast rules, no nonsense? At present, Google continues to thrive in every way as the fastest growing company in the United States, and employees continue to enjoy their work.

A similar scenario occurred in the late 1950s when two groups of scientists, one in the United States and one in Great Britain, competed to solve the enigma of the double helix, the structure of DNA. As it turns out, the Brits—Francis Crick, James Watson, and Maurice Wilkins—won the Nobel Prize for Medicine and Physiology in 1962, in part due to their hard work, but also in part because of their insistence on enjoying some simple pleasures of life—frequent walks along the Cam River in Cambridge, wine tastings, reading good books, discussing British politics, attending movies, and playing occasional games of tennis.[12] If our lives are segmented—work and play—rather than integrated, the center does not hold.

Or consider Karl Barth, whose great labor on his multivolume *Church Dogmatics*, was also aided by listening to Mozart every morning. Reportedly, some ideas even came to him in a dream.[13]

Personal Reflection

How do you view your work and play? Where does sermonizing fit within that scheme? Have you ever talked about "playing with a sermon idea"? Have you ever "worked on your putting" in golf? When do your best ideas occur to you? In your study? On a walk? What does this say about your current way of preparation?

Scriptural Meditation

"Do everything in the name of the Lord Jesus." (Colossians 3:17)

Active Spirituality

I'm sure you've seen the bumper sticker, "Jesus Is Coming, Look Busy!" Or how about H. L. Mencken's definition of puritanism: "the haunting fear that someone, somewhere, may be happy."[14] We laugh at these, but such laughter often masks a deep spiritual need in our lives. It's hardly newsworthy, but a worthy reminder nevertheless, that the word *recreation* means to be "re-created," "to create again." Or in other words, there is more to life than the work we perform, sermonic or otherwise. Holy work or not, there is more to life than pushing harder. As educator Frederic Hudson rightly observes, "An accumulation of doings will actually disempower you if you don't renew your *being* in between doings."[15] Viewing ourselves solely as human *doings*, we feel good about our lives only as we cross items off our "to do" list. Do you know anyone who keeps a "to be" list? I love those lines by Thomas Merton,

> What I do is live
> How I pray is breathe.[16]

Part of our problem lies with how we define spirituality itself, cordoning spiritual matters off from the rest of our earthly existence, treating spirituality as what Brother David Steindl-Rast calls the "penthouse of our existence." Writing from the Benedictine perspective, he rightly notes that spirituality relates to our entire existence. He adds, "Someone will say, 'I come alive when I listen to music,' or 'I come to life when I garden,' or 'I come alive when I play golf.' Wherever we come alive, that is the area in which we are spiritual."[17]

This is something of what Parker Palmer is getting at in *The Active Life*. Palmer maintains that, for more than thirty years now, spirituality has largely been influenced by monastic practices, especially the life and writings of Thomas Merton. These practices include such things as silence, solitude, contemplation, and centeredness. This monastic, or contemplative, model is based largely on a "Not this, but this" approach to spirituality. Fasting means not eating but feasting on God; meditation means not speaking but quietness; solitude means being not in community but alone. These are some of the strengths of the contemplative life, a time away from the normal hustle and bustle.

Do preachers require times of prayer and meditation, reading Scripture and reflecting? Of course we do, the same way plants need water and sunshine, or else they die. But we are more than plants; we are social creatures who desire times of recreation as well. Thus we can integrate monastic and active practices—times of prayer in the study as we wrestle with Sunday's sermon, but also a child's soccer game on a Tuesday night—viewing all of our lives as lived in the presence of God.

Of course, not every minister's spirit is inclined the same way in matters of spirituality. As Palmer notes, "As much as I may need those qualities in my life [fasting, meditation, and so forth], the words do not name those moments when I feel most alive and most able to share life with others."[18] In other words, while fasting can be a deeply moving religious experience, so can a meal with friends. While silence and isolation can affect us in ways unspeakable, literally and figuratively, sharing stories with people we love can be just as powerful. As Simon Tugwell observes in his study of the Order of Preachers in Roman Catholicism, the Dominicans took as their rule of living not the thoroughgoing monastic tradition of Benedict but the rule of Augustine, because it makes no demands that preachers must live lives different from anyone to whom they might preach.[19]

What we often fail to notice with regards to monastic practices, however, especially in terms of sermon preparation, is the very nature of what it means to preach. Namely, all sermons are preached aloud and in community, while most often we prepare them in silence and isolation. Note the disconnect. Maybe we need to question the wisdom of sermon preparation behind closed doors with instructions for holding our calls—although hardly anyone I know actually practices that, despite trying. Still, we spend inordinate amounts of time preparing our sermons in isolation, when maybe more interaction is just what we need. Preacher and teacher Barbara Lundblad goes so far as to suggest preparing sermons in public places, "[A] park bench is a good place to work on sermons because it's full of distractions—like the sound of that train, kids in the sandbox, couples talking up close. . . . Distractions are the stuff of everyday life bumping into scripture texts. I always do at least some of my sermon work in the midst of distractions."[20] I know a minister who occasionally finishes his sermons on his laptop at Starbucks on Saturday nights. Surrounded *by* people, he writes a sermon intended *for* people. Maybe a walk around the park is a way not only to open ourselves up to God's renewing power, but to bring new life to the preparation process itself.

Personal Reflection

What model of spirituality resonates with you? How did your upbringing influence your spirituality? How did your theological training address matters of personal spirituality? Does your approach to sermon preparation fit with your spirituality? Can you imagine preparing a sermon in a public place?

Scriptural Meditation

"You are worried and distracted by many things; there is need of only one thing." (Luke 10:41–42)

_____

_____

_____

_____

_____

_____

_____

_____

_____

_____

_____

Renewal
The Sacrament of Looking

*"The basic command of religion is not 'do this!'
or 'do not do that!' but simply look!"*
—Philip Toynbee[21]

"I've looked at clouds from both sides now."
—Judy Collins

As spiritualist Esther de Waal reminds us, in some traditions morning prayers are called vigils because the first liturgy of the day is "a wake-up call, a call to become vigilant, alert, fully awake, fully alive."[22] Both de Waal and Annie Dillard have devoted whole books—their whole lives really—to the subject of looking.

And both contend that looking is foundational not just to authentic spirituality but to life.

In her Pulitzer Prize–winning *A Pilgrim at Tinker Creek*, Dillard records what she saw one year in nature, inviting readers to join her. Comparing the sights around us with the childhood joy of discovering a penny on the sidewalk, she writes:

> I've been thinking about seeing. There are lots of things to see, unwrapped gifts and free surprises. The world is fairly studded and strewn with pennies cast broadside from a generous hand. But—and this is the point—who gets excited by a mere penny? . . . It is dire poverty indeed when a man is so malnourished and fatigued that he won't stoop to pick up a penny.[23]

Esther de Waal in *Lost in Wonder* echoes a similar call to pay attention. "I found myself astonished," she notes, "when for the first time I picked a daisy and held it under my magnifying glass."[24] Even persons confined to a hospital bed can uncover a world before their eyes with the use of a magnifying glass, de Waal suggests.

Looking is a lost art in this technological world of ours. We surf the Internet at high speed, although rarely fast enough to suit our cravings, failing to note the world right in front of us—a spider web in the corner of the room, the view out the window, the steam circling out of our coffee cup. Technological guru David Gelernter wrestles with this tension in an imaginary conversation between two professors, science versus humanities as it were. The first speaks of technological advance as superior because of its sheer speed and the big picture it enables:

> Did you ever ride at the front of a New York City subway when you were a kid, looking out the front window as the car roars down the track—rocking, screeching like hell, careening round the corners? With the blue tunnel lights batting past? Remember the first time you rode in a plane and it started barreling down the runway? Remember running, when you were a kid, just for the hell of it? Just for fun? *That's progress*. That's *forward motion*.[25]

The other professor, the one with the romantic view of life, concedes that perhaps a fast-paced technological worldview does produce a certain thrill, and maybe it does enable a look at the big picture, but not with any appreciation for the details. The romantic cites as evidence the poet John Ruskin's warning about the coming of the railroads in the nineteenth century:

> There was always more
> in the world
> than men could see,
> walked they ever so slowly;
>
> . . . .
>
> they will see it no better
> for going fast.[26]

I suspect the imaginary professor with the romantic worldview would have loved the real-life professor, John Stilgoe, who teaches History of Landscape at Harvard, the most popular elective on campus. But don't let the title of the course fool you. What Stilgoe really teaches is the art of exploration, which inevitably means walking around with eyes open. Stilgoe invites his students to go exploring, noticing a world hidden not only under manhole covers in the Boston suburbs, but right in front of them. He notes, "I try very hard in this university, which selects students based almost entirely on how well they do with words and numbers, to teach them that there's another way of knowing."[27] He maintains that when we learn to read, to decipher these little marks on the page, much as you're doing now, we simultaneously quit seeing. To demonstrate, he tells his students that almost every child who has not yet learned to read can see something in the Federal Express logo that readers no longer see. Do you see it?

FedEx service marks used by permission

What children who can't read see, and what readers no longer can see, is the arrow. It's between the uppercase *E* and the *x*. Now you see it, don't you? Stilgoe's point: these days we move too fast to see.

Those of us who've preached from Exodus 3, the story of Moses and the burning bush, perhaps recall the importance of "seeing" in the text, which I've highlighted to help us see:

> There the angel of the LORD appeared to [Moses] in a flame of fire out of a bush; he *looked*, and the bush was blazing, yet it was not consumed. Then Moses said, "I must turn aside and *look* at this great sight, and *see* why the bush is not burned up." When the LORD *saw* that he had turned aside to *see*, God called to him out of the bush, "Moses, Moses!" (Exodus 3:2–4, emphasis added)

No wonder those who are devout in their faith are often referred to as "observant."

Preacher Dates
— Take Esther de Waal's advice: get a magnifying glass and look closely at creation
— Look through a telescope at happenings in the night sky
— Stroll through an art gallery, paying attention to the details in at least one piece
— Look long and hard (or long and soft) at the features in another person's face
— Sit in the grass and look closely at the world between those blades of green
— Lie on your back, looking at the clouds overhead, and see what shapes you can spy

> *"When the Muse comes She doesn't tell you to write;*
> *She says get up for a minute, I've something to show you, stand here."*
> —Michael Goldman[28]

The Four Stages
of Preaching

THREE

STAGE ONE: STUDYING
THE SCRIPTURES

"Tough text, huh?"

Do It Again? Already?

In Marilynne Robinson's novel *Gilead*, the Reverend John Ames, a third-generation preacher, reflects on how frequently Sundays come around. In a letter to his son he writes, "When you do this sort of work, it seems to be Sunday all the time, or Saturday night.

You just finish preparing for one week and it's already the next week."[1] Isn't that the truth? Perhaps you've heard the analogy of Sundays coming at us the way telephone poles zip by while we're speeding along on the highway.

Or consider Linda Carolyn Loving's description of the preaching task and having to get ready for yet another Sunday, "If someone who has heard me preach asks me immediately afterwards if I would consider a guest preaching gig or publishing a sermon, I routinely say, 'Not good timing. It's a little like talking to a new mother in the labor room about sex.'"[2]

Whether we're in the mood or not, the Sundays keep coming, always wanting more of us. We may have barely recovered from this week's sermon, and already next week is beckoning. It's enough to wear a poor soul down.

Like it or not, sermons do not magically come together just because we've been eating more ice cream, walking the dog, playing an old guitar. As poet laureate Ted Kooser observes, "It may be lots of fun to sit in a coffeehouse wearing your favorite beret and smoking Camels in a long holder and chatting about poems and poets with your friends, but if you're going to write, you need to go home and write."[3] The first rule of good preaching is having something to say, something *worthwhile* that is. Thus, the verb in the first of the four stages is telling: *studying* the Scriptures. You remember that word *study*, don't you? Think back to college algebra or a church history course in seminary. Studying is hard work; or as the cartoon captures it, "Tough text, huh?" In marriage, life is not always romantic getaways, a glass of wine enjoyed at sunset. Bills have to be paid, the lawn has to be mowed, the clothes and dishes have to be washed. Or in the case of preaching, texts have to be selected and studied.

Still, the demanding aspects of studying in preparation for preaching can be renewing, depending on how we view the task and incorporate it into our lives. Just because we have to work, doesn't mean we can't whistle while we do it. If the way we study is made more appealing, some of the inevitable drudgery can be eased.

The drain of Sunday after Sunday raises a crucial question for us preachers: Whether we are in the mood or not, when do we dare start thinking about next Sunday's sermon? The creative physicist Andrew Cheng observes how, in a profession that consists of both menial tasks and great discoveries—which sounds a lot like the preaching life—it's quite common to experience "a kind of postpartum depression" after finishing one task and waiting to be excited about the next one.[4]

I know ministers who can't even imagine beginning sermon preparation until Tuesday at the earliest, Tuesday afternoon. For some it's more like Wednesday, even Thursday. But not everyone waits. Some feel behind if first thing Monday morning they haven't at least started some commentary work or word study. Some preachers start playing with ideas as early as Sunday evening; yes, the same Sunday evening that follows Sunday morning.

Personal Reflection

When do you normally begin your sermon preparation? What kind of internal signals tell you it's time to move forward and begin preparing the next message? What do you like/dislike about your current rhythm of preparation? Has your approach/rhythm changed over the years? What would you like to do differently?

Scriptural Meditation

"The steadfast love of the LORD never ceases." (Lamentations 3:22)

"P" Is *Not* for Procrastination!

As an INTJ on the Myers-Briggs, I have often joked that P is for procrastination, as opposed to perceiving. Truth be told, we are all different, and those differences affect the way we approach the preparation of sermons, including when we begin. For more than fifteen years now I have listened to seminary students and ministers alike describe their need for a deadline, even if an artificial one. Not everyone, but many of them will announce, "I work best under stress." What I, the dyed-in-the-wool J, want to say in response to such a claim is that sermons, unlike other projects of various sorts, cannot be rushed. When it comes to preparation of sermons, maybe P is for procreation, and sermons need periods of gestation to reach proper birth weight. Too many sermons just aren't ready to be delivered. They're breech or underdeveloped or malnourished. Not yet! The problem? Perhaps we started too late. Why? The answer of course is complicated, and it will vary from person to person, but Julia Cameron claims two things in particular cause us to procrastinate: fear and a misunderstanding of how time and creativity work. Let's look at each of these.

" 'I'm afraid' is always what stands between us and the page," claims Cameron. "When people talk about 'discipline,' they are really talking about how do you get past 'I'm afraid.' " Consider her wisdom, which I've taken the liberty of applying to preaching:

> The fears may not be conscious, and that's what makes it tricky. When we are procrastinating about writing [our sermons] . . . , we are always being backed off by our fears. It may be disguised as our business or our "need to focus" or any number of other distractions, but it boils down to our fear of revealing ourselves to others and ourselves.[5]

God knows we have many fears when it comes to preaching: What if I misrepresent God? What if my sermon bores the listeners? What if folks misunderstand me? What if I trip over my words or, even worse, my preaching robe? You know all those dreams ministers talk about, the ones where we don't have any clothes on in the pulpit. We are a fearful lot. And while these fears relate to the myriad of skills in the overall preaching process, fear is what often keeps us from getting started in the first place. Homiletical burnout may be related to fatigue, but it can also result from the terror of revealing ourselves week after week. It helps to recall that the first word of the resurrection, even prior to the announcement of Christ's being raised, is "Do not be afraid" (Matthew 28:5). What a good word for preachers!

Psychiatrist Rollo May claims that courage is needed to create. He quotes the French artist Edgar Degas, who declared, "A painter paints a picture with the same feeling as that with which a criminal commits a crime."[6] I take that in two ways, recognizing not just the daring and nerve needed, but the elation when a sermon comes together, that we have somehow gotten away with something, bested the system or the muses.

Maybe it is the fear of not being able to find an authentic personal word that has led to so much rampant plagiarism of late, some of it making the headlines. Unable to preach like Barbara Brown Taylor or Fred Craddock, we simply put off preparing until later in the week. There are many legitimate demands upon our time, we reason to ourselves, so we choose to let those things get in the way, and then no one can blame us for the poor quality. "Our minister is not the best preacher, but you can count on him to be there when you're in the hospital." Honestly, must these two aspects of our calling always be at odds? On occasions, sure; but always?

Cameron claims next that when we procrastinate, we do not rightly understand the creativity process. Consider her wisdom, adapted again to apply to preachers:

> A primary reason [preachers] procrastinate is in order to build up a sense of deadline. Deadlines create a flow of adrenaline. Adrenaline medicates and overwhelms the censor. [Preachers] procrastinate so that when they finally get to preparing, they can get past the censor.[7]

She says writers put off starting their essays—preachers put off starting sermon preparation—in hopes that while they are procrastinating, some good ideas will come. We are simply waiting, so goes this line of thinking. "It actually works exactly backward," Cameron notes. "When we start to write, we prime the pump and the flow of ideas begins to move. It is the act of writing that calls ideas forward, not ideas that call forward writing."[8]

The best sermon preparation, like the best writing, takes place in little chunks of time. Ministers who clear a certain day of the week to do large chunks of sermon preparation may find the muses of inspiration do not follow the same schedule. True, some ministers reserve a day near the end of the week, but have been meditating on the text and sermon ideas all along. This approach can be quite effective, though I've heard of some ministers who feel guilty for such a pattern. What a shame. Everyone's rhythm is different; the key is determining if our rhythm works.

When we do not work on the sermon throughout the week, when we delay preparing and then resort to sheer grit and determination, a "Today-is-my-sermon-day-and-one-way-or-another-I'm-going-to-write-today!" mentality, creativity is often stifled rather than nurtured. We become like joggers who foolishly try to put in one long run a week rather than the daily twenty minutes or so.[9]

Ask most people what comes to mind when they hear the word *Saturday*, and you'll see a smile come across their faces. People in business, for instance, who work the standard eight-to-five, Monday-through-Friday week know that Fridays are good and Sundays too, but nothing compared to the ecstasy of Saturdays, the day between the end of one week and the beginning of another.

Ask most ministers what comes to mind when they hear the word *Saturday*, and the results will not be fit to print. Where are the "Saturdays" in the rhythm of our weeks?

Personal Reflection

In what ways does your approach to studying the Scriptures require discipline? In what ways do you prepare with a sense of joy and adventure? What are your fears when it comes to preaching week in and week out? How do you schedule sermon preparation? What are your Saturdays like?

Scriptural Meditation

"Do not be alarmed." (Mark 16:6)

Fred Craddock's Two Chairs

If we are honest, we will have to acknowledge there are aspects of sermon preparation that do indeed require discipline as well as aspects that call for more creativity. This is where I find Fred Craddock's approach so helpful. Craddock insists that sermons should be prepared in two distinct phases, each of them with its own unique purposes. He claims ministers should frame and mount this statement somewhere prominent in their study: "The process of arriving at something to say is to be distinguished from the process of determining how to say it." Or perhaps we could mount another of his statements on our wall: "Unless the minister has two eurekas, it is not likely the listeners will have one."[10]

The two processes correspond to the exegetical and homiletical tasks of sermon preparation, which Craddock claims are so different they might actually be done best in different chairs. The exegetical chair is wooden, straight-backed, and hard. Exegetical work is just that—work! The homiletical chair is soft, comfortable, and inviting. In the softer chair we brainstorm, giving ourselves permission for flights of fancy. But not in the wooden chair. There is work to be done.

Believe it or not, the space in which we work affects the kind of work we do there. In her book *The Writer's Desk*, a fascinating collection of photographs and interviews, Jill Krementz portrays the varied spaces in which writers work, no two of them the same. Stephen King in jeans and tennis shoes, with his feet on the desk and a dog beneath his chair. Eudora Welty with perfect posture at a perfectly organized desk. Mona Simpson with a laptop and her feet up on a small wooden table. John Irving in a neatly organized space, lit by four windows. E. B. White in what looks like a boat house, with the simplest wooden desk and a typewriter. Richard Ford never in the same space, working wherever his life takes him (He says, "My 'desk' is more of a concept than a thing. It's like the 'Belize desk' at the State Department; an idea more than a place you actually sit at."). Robert Penn Warren in what could pass for Thoreau's cabin at Walden, very crude. Toni Morrison on a couch with a small notebook and pen. For John Updike, who wrote the introduction to Krementz's book, "What is crucial is a sense of ease that frees the mind. And yet the atmosphere should not be so easy as to discourage a day's worth of uphill work."[11]

Personally, I was always convinced better sermons could be written at rolltop desks. Come to find out, it's not true; but I love my desk nonetheless. I bought the antique several years ago now from a church I formerly served as interim minister. More recently I also restored a church pew—one of those sawed-off versions—which serves as guest seating in my study. I bought an area rug and some matching curtains as well. Equally important, I displayed some of my favorite golf memorabilia, including an autographed picture of Phil Mickelson at the 2004 Masters that my good friend Lynn Horak got for me. And I bought a comfortable chair! Yes, I finally took Craddock's advice literally. There are moments in my week when I sit at my desk, as I do now. There are other moments when with laptop, or a book, or a pad of paper I sit in the comfortable chair.

The space in which we work makes a difference, especially when it comes to the creative work of sermon preparation. As a guest minister I visit lots of different spaces that pastors work in.

Some of them resemble a prison cell more than a study: cinder-block walls painted ghastly colors, floors with bare linoleum. For relatively little money most spaces can be transformed, much the way college students transform their barren dorm rooms. Even a green plant or two can make a difference. Call such touches "preacherly comforts."

I know one pastor who has two spaces in his church from which he works, one an office located in the usual place, with phone, computer, and a space for receiving folks. But the other space is a study. He found an unused room in the education wing of the church into which he moved his books and a desk, along with some "preacherly comforts" of his own. He says he feels different in that space.

One of the most memorable studies in a church I've seen has been designed to resemble a kitchen. The woman pastor did most of her studying at her kitchen table before the church, a new start, could build office space. When it came time to design her study at the church, they purchased a large rectangular kitchen table with a stressed antique look and curtains that have a kitchenlike feel to them. She joked, "I'm not sure how the next minister will feel about this if he's a man." Who knows? What's important is how she feels in that space now, and how we feel about ours.

Personal Reflection

Where do you sit to prepare your sermons? Is the space at the church and/or your home conducive to creativity? What do you call the space at your church? Office? Study? Can you imagine using different spaces for different kinds of work? What kinds of different spaces might you try?

"God saw everything that [God] had made, and indeed, it was very good." (Genesis 1:31)

Renewal
The Sacrament of Walking

"Perhaps the truth depends on a walk around the park."
—Wallace Stevens

"It is solved by walking."
—Augustine

Although I have no idea of the context in which he said it, Augustine believed walking could solve "it." I like to think he was referring to preaching, the weekly struggle to put sermons together. After all, Augustine was the church's first homiletician, a bishop who preached countless sermons. Walking does indeed solve many things, but even when it doesn't, walking is one of God's good gifts in life.

In *Wanderlust*, her fascinating book on the history of walking,

Rebecca Solnit describes walking in terms of three characters coming together in conversation—the mind, the body, and the world. "Walking allows us to be in our bodies and in the world without being made busy by them. It leaves us free to think without being wholly lost in our thoughts."[12] Solnit suspects "that the mind, like the feet, works at about three miles an hour. If this is so, then modern life is moving faster than the speed of thought, or thoughtfulness."[13] Walking often produces insights we would not otherwise have, claims Julia Cameron. "We use the phrase 'body of knowledge,' and that phrase is quite literal. Our body has knowledge to give us—that, and inspiration."[14]

Prior to William and Dorothy Wordsworth, walking had never really been an acceptable leisure-time activity. What had once been undertaken only as a means of inferior transportation slowly but surely became recreational, a slowing down of one's life.[15] Today, most Americans who walk primarily do so for exercise, a purpose-driven approach, while on any given Sunday in Great Britain more than eighteen million people head to the country simply to enjoy the beauty.[16]

Not surprisingly, Henry David Thoreau was an avid walker. He claimed that walking "comes only by the grace of God. It requires a direct dispensation from Heaven to become a walker."[17] Walking is indeed one of God's gifts to us. In fact, as Thoreau noted, the verb "to saunter" actually comes from the term for Holy Land, *Sainte Terre*. Isn't that something? Even on our most casual walks, "we saunter toward the Holy Land."[18]

Maybe the "it" that walking solves, according to Augustine, is not our sermons but us preachers.

Preacher Dates
— Spend half a day at the zoo, taking in some of the creatures who walk on fours
— Note the sights as you walk part of a route you normally drive in your neighborhood
— If you already have a walking route, try traversing it in reverse
— Park between stores at a strip mall and walk rather than drive between them
— Recall your favorite nature verses from the Bible while walking in a remote area

— Take a dog on a walk; borrow one if you have to
— Pay attention to the trees on a favorite walking path
— Get to a beach, or a mountain, or a park, and go for a walk

"In my room, the world is beyond my understanding;
But when I walk I see that it consists of three or four hills, and a cloud."
—Wallace Stevens[19]

"I only went out for a walk, and finally concluded to stay out
till sundown, for going out, I found, was really going in."
—John Muir[20]

Giving Sermons the Time of Day

Not just *where* we sit, but *when* we sit, to prepare our sermons is a serious concern. Everyone is different, and so are some weeks for that matter. We cannot always count on uninterrupted blocks of time, and as we considered in the introduction, maybe that's for the best. As the old saying goes, ministry is in the interruptions. Still, the time of day we prepare our sermons matters. Some of us do better work in the mornings than late afternoons. Some do their best creative thinking late at night when most people are fast asleep. What is essential is that we be comfortable with our own idiosyncrasies. The writer Philip Roth recalls a line by Joyce Carol Oates, who claims that "when writers ask each other what time they start working and when they finish and how much time they take for lunch, they're actually trying to find out, 'Is he as crazy as I am?'" Roth adds, "I don't need that question answered."[21]

Julia Cameron tells about an artist she knows who actually schedules his day imitating a "schoolboy's schedule—English in second period, math in third, lunch break in fourth, biology in fifth, etc."[22] This may seem a bit rigid for some, reminiscent of a ruler across the hand when you were caught acting up in class. Still, there is something to be said for a plan, even a flexible one at that. It takes a certain measure of discipline to prepare our sermons, or else we fall prey to what has been called "the tyranny of the urgent," when whatever catches our eye is what we're onto next.

Personal Reflection

How do you break up the week between exegetical and homiletical concerns? How do you schedule the hours of your day? Where does sermonizing best fit?

Scriptural Meditation

"And there was evening and there was morning." (Genesis 1:31)

Poet or Scholar?

Most of us are too busy getting ready for Sunday's sermon — among other tasks — to assess whether the way we are getting ready really works. *Who has time to think about our approach to preaching? We're thinking about a sermon!* We know better of course than to assume that all preachers go about the task of sermon preparation uniformly. Teachers of preaching may suggest certain approaches, but over time every preacher finds his or her own way.

Kathleen Norris offers a wonderful distinction between two of those ways in general—the way of the poet and the way of the scholar. When she was in college, Norris was just beginning to test her poetic abilities. One day, sitting around the commons with some other students and one young professor out to prove himself, Norris dared to share that she was working on a poem about angels. The professor, a recent PhD grad from Columbia, dismissed the idea right off. He said she couldn't possibly write a poem on angels without having read a whole list of books, which he then began to name. The usually shy Norris would not be put off: "No. First I have to write the poem, and then I will look at the books." She goes on to say that in that very moment "the world had just opened up for me: I had identified an essential difference between the poet and the scholar, and knew for certain which ground to claim as mine."[23]

The difference between poet and scholar, according to Norris, has to do with the order in which we approach our task. Applied to preaching, I think about the common homiletical advice of meditating, praying, and brainstorming before ever opening a commentary. This advice is so common, in hermeneutics and homiletics alike, that some ministers I know feel guilty for not following it. Myself included—or at least I used to feel bad about it. But Norris names the key difference between the two approaches: order. Some ministers need to avoid the commentaries early on in the process, true. For others, a quick peek at the exegetical issues serves as a helpful jump start.

I remember dropping in on a minister friend one afternoon in the middle of the week. We visited briefly, then I asked how his sermon was coming. As I recall, he was stuck. In typical fashion, I asked what text he was preaching and what the commentaries had to say about the passage. He hadn't looked there yet. For me, I need an early peek, but not everyone. Or perhaps some weeks our approach will vary.

Personal Reflection

Do you think of your approach to preparation more as poet or scholar? What other term might you prefer over studying? Exploring? How do you begin your own preparation? Are there certain sources that help more than others early on? Are there some that hinder? Does your approach vary from week to week? On what do the changes depend? Nature of your week? Nature of the text? Something else?

Scriptural Meditation

"*By wisdom a house is built.*" (*Proverbs 24:3*)

_____

_____

_____

_____

_____

_____

_____

_____

_____

_____

_____

The Devil in the Details?

Recently a middle-aged woman warned me at the beginning of the semester that she was going to struggle with homiletics class. She was right. It wasn't a fear of public speaking or trouble finding stories or crafting the sermon itself. No, she knew herself well enough from her biblical studies classes to realize she would get stuck in the text. In other words, the first stage would be so demanding—so delightful really—she would be unable to quit studying. As I said, she was right. Her sermons were not completed on time because there were still exegetical issues she'd unearthed in recent journal articles she needed to ponder.

For some ministers, studying the Scriptures is such sheer

delight that they overdo it. They can't free themselves from the task. In my first pastorate a colleague from another nearby church wanted to borrow one of my Greek exegetical commentaries. He said, "I'm preaching through Ephesians this year, and I can't decide if this one preposition is a locative of sphere or instrumental of means." Believe it or not, I refrained from commenting at the time. Good thing, because I now realize my first instinct captures only half the picture. True, getting bogged down in that much detail seems to be overkill, but I have to admit it does my heart some good to know that there are still ministers who study the Scriptures in some detail.

Most of us know ministers at both extremes: they either get bogged down in the details, unable to escape, or their approach to preaching doesn't seem to include any serious exegetical work at all. What's the saw about ditches on both sides of the road? More important, however, than the tendencies of our colleagues is recognizing our own tendencies. Sociologist Barry Schwartz refers to the difference between maximizers and satisficers, using the example of a woman buying a sweater.[24] If she is a maximizer, it's not enough that she has found an attractive sweater that fits, and for a good price. There could be a better sweater at another store—maybe the identical item, but for less. Or maybe another, more comfortable one. Or maybe . . . You get the idea. In contrast, satisficers don't settle for any old sweater, but they seem to recognize a good thing when they find it.

I know preachers—you probably do too—who simply can't settle for what they have found already. There might be more details worth examining. These preachers remind me of the weatherman in the Dallas/Ft. Worth area, where I attended seminary. Every evening at 5:00, 6:00, and 10:00 this man would begin the weather report with the jet stream analysis. He would debate the merits of readings taken at 33,000 feet versus those taken at 34,000 feet. He would note changing patterns in the plains states, pointing out jet stream currents as strong as 200 miles per hour. After several minutes of the jet stream analysis, he would ask, "What effect is this going to have on our weather? I don't think it's going to affect us." So every day at 5:00, 6:00, and 10:00 I would talk back to the television, "Then why tell us about it?"

The reason, of course, was that this weatherman loved weather. Well, not weather, but meteorology. Most of us love weather, especially good weather. This man loved the study of weather. It happens with preachers, too. Some of us love not just God, but the study of God, theology. But people tune into sermons for the same reason they tune into the weather report—to hear a relevant word. Alas, some ministers get stuck in the details.[25]

On the other end of the spectrum are those whose standards are too low. They settle for a quick read, a surface-level interpretation. As a result, listeners hear sermons with little or no thought given to them. Imagine a weather report with no details. Or to reference the shopping metaphor, imagine a shabbily dressed sermon, plaids and stripes hastily thrown together.

The preacher in the middle, the satisficer, has learned that neither extreme is wise, that study is necessary but not too much. Having worked hard at the exegetical process, she is satisfied. I love the image homiletics professor Stephen Farris uses for realistic levels of exegesis in the pastorate. He recalls an episode of M*A*S*H in which Charles Emerson Winchester has just arrived on the front line. He's a meticulous surgeon, one who knows the finer points of his profession; but he's slow, very slow, and soldiers are dying. Colonel Potter pulls Winchester out of the operating room, ordering Hawkeye to take over. Potter explains to the prima donna that in a situation like this they do "meatball surgery." There's no time for anything else. Farris suggests that "meatball exegesis" is what ministers must do in the church.[26] Sunday is coming and the assignment is neither a formal exegetical paper nor an impromptu devotional thought.

Personal Reflection

What are your own tendencies when it comes to studying? Do you enjoy it? Do you enjoy it to a fault? Do you have a tendency to stay on a surface level? Do you avoid studying? How might you find a better balance in your approach?

"You shall love the Lord your God with all your heart." (Mark 12:30)

A Balanced Diet of Sources

Amazingly, we are influenced not just by our own study habits but by the kinds of resources available that lend themselves to the extremes. Although it's only a spoof on certain kinds of commentaries, the following excerpt hits close to home in some cases:

Verse 1: "Jack and Jill went up the hill, to fetch a pail of water."

The word "and" presents some difficulties which are not apparent to the casual reader. There is considerable doubt in the minds of most scholars as to whether Jack was stimulated to undertake this mission by a basic need for water. Since most functions in the home involving water, such as cooking, washing clothes, scrubbing floors, etc., are normally undertaken by the distaff side, it is widely held that the force of "and" in this context probably means that Jack set out with a strong picture image of Jill in his mind, and several existentialist scholars also insist that her parting words were undoubtedly ringing in his ears.[27]

Recently, my New Testament colleague David May showed me a similar penchant in a legitimate commentary on 1 and 2 Timothy, part of a series. The research was thorough, to be sure, but of no practical help whatsoever for preaching. While I am grateful for scholars, even those who unearth the esoteric, pastors need resources that work for their purposes. Think of it like this, there are some sources written with both eyes on the ancient biblical world and some sources written with both eyes on the pulpit, including prepackaged illustrations and sermon outlines. But there are others, and they are a minority to be sure, who write with one eye on the text and the other on the church—sources such as *Interpretation* (John Knox Press), *The New Interpreter's Bible* (Abingdon Press), and the more recent *New Cambridge Bible Commentary* (Cambridge University Press), to name just a few. We would do well to check out these kinds of sources, to see if they work for our own approach to studying. If you live near a theological seminary, use the library before investing a lot of money. Not all commentaries are created equal, even within a given series.

We should also note how outdated some commentaries are. My New Testament colleague likes to make this point by showing his students a picture of Matthew Henry:

Matthew Henry's commentary continues to be popular with some ministers even though he died in 1714. It's the date of republication that misleads some preachers. Can you imagine the kinds of medical practice used at that time, more than fifty years before America declared independence? Can you imagine the approach to dentistry? Some older works still have merit, but some biblical study aids are no longer useful; they have run their course.

Personal Reflection

What kinds of study aids do you currently use? Have any of them become outdated? When was the last time you considered purchasing a new commentary? Is there money in your church's budget for a book allowance? Do you ever visit a theological library near you?

Scriptural Meditation

"You shall love the Lord your God . . . with all your mind." (Mark 12:30)

Renewal
The Sacrament of Napping

"How lovely it is to rest and then do nothing afterwards."
— Spanish Proverb

It goes without saying that most preaching books do not have chapters on napping, unless of course it has to do with how to keep parishioners awake on Sunday mornings. I'm told that in the Rule of St. Benedict provisions were made for what to do if a monk were to fall asleep during one of the hours of worship. Benedict's advice: Let him sleep; he may need the rest more than the time of prayer. I love that story. Napping is such a grand and glorious gift of God.

Unfortunately, napping is one of those great childhood privileges that most of us surrendered when we graduated from kindergarten. If we have young children or grandchildren, we read them to sleep for an afternoon nap, but rarely allow ourselves the same indulgence. The implication is that napping is something you outgrow. How sad! Barbara Holland, author of *Endangered Pleasures*, notes that "people deprived of daylight and their wristwatches, with no notion of whether it was day or night, sink blissfully asleep in midafternoon as regular as clocks."[28]

In our full-speed-ahead world, those who do take an occasional nap are often seen as slackers. According to the World Nap Organization — yes, there is such an organization! — nearly 40 percent of nappers feel guilty for indulging in a little shut-eye. Properly understood, napping is countercultural, revolutionary in a fashion. In *The Art of the Siesta*, Thierry Paquot writes, "The siesta is a means for us to reclaim our own time, outside the clockmaster's control. The siesta is our liberator."[29]

A few years ago a friend sent me a story about the countercultural life and napping. It's one of those e-mail pieces that makes the rounds, so you may have seen this one. It's the story of a Mexican fisherman who midmorning was unloading his fishing boat when an American businessman on vacation asked how long it took to catch the fish. "Only a little while," the fisherman said. The American was incredulous. He wanted to know why the man didn't stay out longer and catch more. The fisherman said he could but didn't see the point. He said, "I sleep late, fish a little, play with my children, and in the afternoon take siesta with my wife Maria. I have a full life."

The businessman tried to show him how if he caught more he could expand the business, buy more boats, hire other fishermen, eventually make millions. "Millions?" the fisherman asked, "Then what?" The American replied, "That's the best part. You could retire. Sleep late, fish a little, play with your kids, and take siestas with your wife."

Even the word *siesta* invites us into another way of being in the world. Paquot employs a whole series of wonderful terms to describe the siesta—words like seductive, alluring, tender, irresistible, warm. He writes, "Your body, which was weighing you down just a moment before, now seems progressively lighter, invisible, non-existent. Happiness—or a form of happiness—overwhelms you. Let yourself be, let yourself go and, with surprise, surrender yourself."[30]

Preacher Dates
— Close this book and your eyes for a few minutes; the world will spin without you
— Start a tradition of napping on Saturdays or better yet, Sundays after services
— Get away to a park or beach and treat yourself to a catnap in the sunshine
— Designate a favorite couch or chair as your nap zone, and claim a nap now and then
— Read a book to kids or grandkids at nap time and join them

> *"[A nap is] any rest period up to twenty minutes' duration involving unconsciousness but not pajamas."*
> —Wilse Webb[31]

Two Roads Diverged

I remember some years ago hearing Eugene Lowry announce that if you had told him at the beginning of his ministry that United Methodists would one day embrace the use of the lectionary for preaching, he would have declared you crazy. He said this at a time when Methodists were using the lectionary regularly, as many still do, but when this was not the case in some other traditions. In fact, I remember thinking, *Well, maybe the Methodists and the Presbyterians, but never the Baptists and Disciples of Christ.* Reminds me of the fellow who back in the early 1960s predicted the Beatles would never amount to anything.

What is amazing just a few years later is how many ministers would never dream of departing from the lectionary. Well, that, and the number of preachers who for various reasons still refuse to consider it at all. As for the latter group, perhaps their Protestant blood enjoys protesting anything remotely Roman Catholic. (Protestants are protestors by nature.) Never mind that the Judaism of Jesus' day observed a lectionary of readings from the Torah and Prophets. Some even see evidence of a Jewish lectionary in Luke's story of Jesus at the synagogue in Nazareth. If you happen to find yourself in this doubter's corner, Eugene Lowry's little book *Living with the Lectionary* and Shelley Cochran's *The Pastor's Underground Guide to the Revised Common Lectionary* are both excellent resources.[32] There really are very good reasons to consider the lectionary. After all, the passages come from the Bible!

As for those who never depart from the lectionary, it might do us some good to consider all the passages in the Bible not included in most versions of the lectionary. In fact, it would be interesting—probably depressing, too—if we were to flip through the pages of a Bible, an actual leatherbound copy of tissue-thin paper, but one that included only the lectionary texts. Can you say "pocket-sized"?

When you think about the repetition of the same passages every three years, over and over again, it's like trying to imagine navigating a large city but being restricted to only a portion of the streets and highways available. There are other spots to see, other experiences to be had in the great city called Bible. Sometimes the less-traveled road has some surprises in store.

When introducing the Revised Common Lectionary to seminarians, I often joke, "Try it. If you don't like it, don't use it. There's no such thing as lectionary police!" Wrong! I didn't think such a thing existed until on the Sunday after September 11, when I informed the church where I would be preaching that I planned to depart from that week's suggested readings, opting instead for Jesus' Beatitudes in Matthew 5, the blessings of our Lord for a hurting people. The associate minister kept repeating, "We use the lectionary passages here." I told her I realized that, but this did seem a fitting time to depart from such a practice. "We use the lectionary passages here," was all she could say.

Some churches do indeed "use the lectionary passages here." Some do not. And while a local congregation's traditions and/or a denomination's approach are not to be dismissed out of hand, it might be wise to reflect on how many ministers have either refused to consider using the lectionary or have cycled through it so many times the Bible's rich diversity has gone flat.

Personal Reflection

What are your own views on the use of the lectionary? Your church's? Are there times you find it surprisingly relevant? Are there times you find it a hindrance?

Scriptural Meditation

"The wind blows where it chooses." (John 3:8)

How Long, O Lord?

Almost every minister has heard the bromide about spending an hour in the study for every minute in the pulpit. If such advice were put into practice, my guess is church folks would be eating lunch a little earlier most Sundays. No doubt about it, such advice is naive. There is not enough time, and besides, there is hardly any reason to spend twenty hours—more or less—preparing a sermon.

Far too many guilt trips have been laid upon far too many of us. I recall a friend telling me about the great privilege of studying under George Buttrick near the end of his ministry. One day Buttrick had just finished lecturing on how to study for sermons, an elaborate and demanding task as he laid it out, when a student asked, "Dr. Buttrick, how would you propose doing that for those of us who have to preach more than one sermon per week?" His answer is telling: "You can only preach one sermon per week. Period. And this is what's required."

Recalling that advice, I think about the great Presbyterian preacher's son, homiletician David Buttrick, who claims that "ministers must study every day of their lives." He continues, "They can. They can because laypeople can manage churches very well, design programs, write church newspapers and all the rest."[33] Both Buttricks are right, up to a point. It's true too many ministers allow demands to interrupt their study time, but let's think for a moment about the quality of our study time, not just the quantity.

Imagine if someone were to offer you an additional week of preparation time but require no more time than you already give to your sermons. Twice as much time without any more commitment on your part. Sounds too good to be true, doesn't it, like a used car salesman promising the impossible. Actually, the system I'm proposing does exactly this. It simply asks that you begin your sermon preparation one week earlier and stagger the Sundays. Let me explain.

Most weeks ministers follow a plan that can be described as follows: Between now—whenever "now" is—and Sunday, I must decide on a biblical text, study that passage, find some illustrations, give some kind of thought to the arrangement of the materials I've gathered, print the manuscript/get notes ready, and be ready to preach. In other words, the four stages as I'm calling them, all crammed into six days, less really. Granted, some preachers do advanced planning, but planning and preparation are not the same thing.

But what if this familiar process of putting sermons together were spread out over two weeks' time? In other words, take the amount of time you currently spend in preparation and simply divide it over thirteen days or so. The way it works is simple, but the dividends are surprisingly rich. Recall Fred Craddock's dictum that fundamental to sermon preparation is recognizing two distinct phases, the exegetical and homiletical, each requiring its own eureka moments. If we let the two weeks of preparation correspond to these two distinct tasks, it would look something like this:[34]

Week 1:

	Monday	Tuesday	Wednesday	Thursday	Friday	Saturday	Sunday
AM	homiletics	homiletics	homiletics	homiletics			
PM		exegetical		exegetical			

Week 2:

	Monday	Tuesday	Wednesday	Thursday	Friday	Saturday	Sunday
AM	homiletics	homiletics	homiletics	homiletics			
PM		exegetical		exegetical			

The exegetical work done in week one, whenever it occurs, is the beginning of sermon preparation for the Sunday of week two. The homiletical work in week two begins not from scratch, but by building on the exegetical framework begun the week before. What time of day and how often can be tailored to any person's own rhythms. The important thing is that ministers allow themselves twice as much time to live with the sermon while no more actual preparation time is required.

Notice, two sermons are being prepared during any one week, but how that works is important. In my own adaptation of this approach, I generally do exegetical work in fairly large chunks, say an hour or so on Tuesday and Thursday afternoons, as the chart shows. Exegesis does not require much creativity, and trust me, after lunch I'm not very creative. My most creative time of day is the mornings, and thus in week two I work at—or is that "play with"?—the homiletical task in little doses every morning, sometimes as little as fifteen minutes. I prefer to finish the exegetical work by Thursday of week one so I don't confuse the two sermons.

During the first week the task is to do the exegetical homework. No sermon ideas are required. If they come, fine. Even so, I write those ideas down on another piece of paper. My task in week one is exegetical. Come week two, I can pick up the exegetical notes, and whatever homiletical scribbles I've made, and begin the creative task of putting the sermon together.

Personal Reflection

How much time do you normally spend on sermon preparation? Does that very question threaten you? Does your current approach work well? What is your reaction to the two-week approach? If it doesn't seem right for you, what alternative might work better for you?

Scriptural Meditation

"May the grace of our Lord Jesus Christ be with your spirit." (Galatians 6:18)

Adjusting the Focus

The final phase of stage one is deciding what the sermon will be about. Here, exegesis begins to yield to homiletics. We turn the corner from ancient text to modern world. At some point we must decide what our sermon will try to accomplish. This is no easy task, not just because of the many needs present in any given congregation on any given Sunday, but because every text in Scripture has so many different meanings. Granted, not everything prefaced by the words "The Bible says . . ." is credible, but texts are elastic, alive with possibilities.

For instance, we read a story in Mark's Gospel about Jesus and his inner circle—best friends?—of Peter, James, and John going up a mountain. There, Jesus is gloriously transfigured, while the three onlookers are befuddled. Meanwhile, down below the other nine disciples are trying to figure out how to help a father who has brought his ill son to be cured (Mark 9:2–29). What will the sermon on this text be about this week? The possibilities are not limitless, but they are numerous. Of course as important as deciding what a sermon *will* be about is deciding what a sermon will *not* be about. We only have twenty minutes or so. We can't possibly begin to uncover all of the wealth in any one passage in any one sermon. We're not talking about a Bible study from the pulpit, but a sermon. Besides, research shows that an overload of competing messages is often lost on people.[35]

Far too many sermons are preached in the spirit of Rev. Boling and his "infamous tangents" as seen in the cartoon above.

I can imagine a listener chiming in, "Off the preacher goes to who-knows-where. Just wake me up when it's over." So how then do we keep our listeners with us, or maybe more accurately, how do we stay with our listeners?

One image for this stage of sermon preparation is that of a movie director who must decide which scenes stay and which ones end up on the floor of the editing room. Like DVDs with their deleted scenes, preachers who omit certain textual aspects will have opportunities for conversation with parishioners who wish to discuss texts more at length another time.

Or perhaps a better image than director is gardener. H. Grady Davis popularized this metaphor for preaching. In the late 1950s,

Two thirds of the way into his sermon, Rev. Boling goes off on another of his infamous tangents.

at a time when many preaching books used the language of construction—a left-brained, male-dominant image—Davis dared to compare a sermon to a tree, "a living organism" with roots and blossoms. He even went so far as to introduce the word *design* to homiletics in his book *Design for Preaching*.[36] Perhaps more important than finding things to say on Sunday, adding a plank here, another there, is pruning the sermon's many ideas down to one manageable idea or focus.

Personal Reflection

How do you decide what a sermon will be about? How do you decide what a sermon will *not* be about? Think about this week's sermon. As director, what artistic decisions need to be made? Or how does the idea of pruning a tree speak to you? Think of another metaphor you might use in your design of sermons.

Scriptural Meditation

> *"O the depth of the riches and wisdom and knowledge of God!"*
> *(Romans 11:33)*

Pet Peeves—Who, Me?

I remember my first preaching professor, Al Fasol, challenging us students to look back through six months' worth of sermons sometime, earmarking the ones in which the sole focus was a challenge we issued. In his experience, he said, it was rare for preachers to announce good news; they more often resorted to what he called "pulpit pounding." Worse than that, he continued, is the sad fact that all too often the challenge issued is one of the preacher's pet peeves—maybe harping on sexual sins the way certain televangelists did a few years back, or maybe raising social justice issues related to world hunger, but pet peeves nonetheless.

The range of sermon purposes is immense. Sometimes our aim is more cognitive than active, calling for reflection and thoughtful pondering. Other times the focus calls for a response, something to be changed either personally or in society. In contemporary homiletics, other sermon approaches seek to evoke an experience, not necessarily to the neglect of reflection and action, but an experience nonetheless. In a recent collection of essays entitled *The Purposes of Preaching*, contributors name some of the broader aims of preaching, ten in all.[37]

If the range of possibilities is so great, why the narrowness of so much of our preaching? Think, for instance, about two basic aims of preaching, what James Sanders calls "prophetic" and "constitutive." The former, just as it sounds, is a "prophetic critique" of the status quo. The latter is more supportive, that which *constitutes* life under God's good grace.[38] The one speaks in the imperative—the ought-ness of Scripture: "We ought to love our neighbors." The other speaks in the indicative—the is-ness of Scripture: "God loves us unconditionally." I have written elsewhere about our penchant for the prophetic to the neglect of the gospel's good news,[39] but what concerns me here is how we determine what our sermons will be about, how much of our sermonic focus is self-determined. I think about that mantra repeated on so many seminary campuses across North America, "It's not about you. It's not about you!" If the message of our preaching is not about us, how shall we decide the agenda of our sermon topics?

Personal Reflection

In what ways do you perceive your own agenda crowding out the multifaceted aspects of Scripture? What would a more balanced approach to determining a sermon's purpose look like? Do you ever seek congregational input? What kinds of sermons do you preach most often, challenging or comforting? Are you certain of your answer?

Scriptural Meditation

> "O LORD, my heart is not lifted up, my eyes are not raised too high." (Psalm 131:1)

FOUR

STAGE TWO:
BRAINSTORMING STORIES

"I'd like to introduce the fellow who's behind all those sermon illustrations that begin with 'A man once said to me . . .'"

The Gospel and Groucho

Every eighteen months or so I teach a weeklong course on narrative preaching as part of the MTh Program at Spurgeon's College in London, England. A few years ago I had a free Sunday afternoon and evening for sightseeing. I'd seen a notice that the respected scholar N. T. Wright would be preaching that Sunday evening at Westminster Abbey. A couple of seminary students and I attended the service. It was a Sunday evening, so attendance was down. So small, in fact, worshipers sat in the chancel area between the opposing choir stalls. Still, the service was formal in its own way, with processional and all of the prescribed liturgy for the day.

At the appropriate moment, N. T. Wright stood to read the Gospel lesson, then began his homily. I will never forget his first two words: "Groucho Marx." In that grand place the first words of this scholar's sermon were "Groucho Marx." Wright began his sermon with a story about when the humorist was asked on his seventieth birthday how he would want to be thought of in a hundred years. Groucho's response? "In remarkably good condition for someone his age." It was a funny story, but what struck me at the time, and still does, is the audacity by which we preachers juxtapose readings from ancient Scripture with quotes by Groucho Marx and others like him.

Week after week, we study the Scriptures in hopes of finding a message for the church—stage one—then begin to consider contemporary connections, how that message relates to today and what stories we might use to make that relationship clear—stage two. We dare to believe that a line from Groucho Marx, an image from Flannery O'Connor, a scene from a Spielberg flick, even a story from our own lives, can somehow relate to the proclamation of the gospel.

I have come to the conviction that the term "biblical preaching" is both redundant and incomplete. It is *redundant* because the biblical message is what we preach, God's redemptive acts and hope for humanity.[1] It is *incomplete* because spouting ancient Scripture is never enough. We must make connections with our day, or else we have not really preached! Most preachers and teachers of preaching would agree—*most*, but not all. In the last fifty years or so, a good number of theologians and preaching professors have been debating the making of such connections, most especially when those connections take place via stories. It is not the preacher's job to make God relevant via our stories, they argue.[2]

For most of us, however, sermons that blend the ancient and contemporary are the norm. In part, because God continues to speak in literature, life, and a myriad of other ways. And also in part, because as preachers we instinctively recognize barren places in our sermons, dry spots in the wilderness that call out for stories. Whether or not we would pit the finer points of Emil Brunner and Paul Tillich over against the likes of Karl Barth and Hans Frei, most of us look for stories to sprinkle liberally throughout our messages. Besides, the very same Karl Barth who claimed sermons don't need illustrations used them in his own preaching, even if he later regretted it on occasion.[3]

Still, I have known ministers who for various reasons reached a point in their ministries where they refused to include illustrations in their preaching. Maybe they resented the burden of finding stories for Sunday's sermon. A friend and colleague from my PhD days, who was also studying homiletics, finally had it with the demands of seeking stories. "Why can't we just preach the word," he asked one day, "instead of always trying to keep folks interested? Isn't the text enough?" Not surprisingly, he later recanted of that position. Still, he was right about one thing: the burden of finding stories week in and week out can tax the best of us.

I also remember a female student at the seminary who, when asked by her peers why her sermon had not contained even one contemporary story, came to a sudden realization. In tears, she recalled how her former husband always interrupted her if she tried to tell a story or joke. "I'll tell it," he would say. "You don't know how to tell stories."

And I think of all the preachers I've talked to who admitted not using many illustrations because the pastors they grew up hearing used way too many, story after story without much textual presence or much of a point for that matter. The opposite can also be true—ministers using far too few stories—resulting in a kind of knee-jerk reaction approach to illustrating their sermons.

Personal Reflection

What are your own views regarding the use of stories in preaching? Do you consider them a necessity or concession? How have your views of storytelling in preaching been conditioned by your theological education? Your peers? Your mentors? Your upbringing? Do you consider yourself a storyteller?

Scriptural Meditation

> *"[Jesus] did not speak to them except in parables." (Mark 4:34)*

Getting Personal

In homiletics one of the more recent debates has focused not so much on whether contemporary stories and illustrations are appropriate in general, but more specifically whether *personal* stories belong in the pulpit at all.[4] Does the preacher's recounting of a trek to an antique store on a Saturday afternoon belong in Sunday morning's sermon right alongside the words of prophets and apostles? What about a recent attempt at running a marathon next to words from Jesus on perseverance? Is the preacher entitled to remind us of life's fragility by means of his own close encounter with another automobile on the highway?

David Buttrick laid down as law his own aversion to personal stories. Not every pastor waded through his volume *Homiletic*, but even for those who didn't, news of his dictum against personal stories caught the attention of many. In short, he argued that personal illustrations distract listeners from their intended purpose—to illustrate. So instead of getting the point, Buttrick argued, listeners find their attention divided between the point and some insight into the preacher's own life. His solution? "Locate the illustration in the common consciousness" of listeners. Rather than tell about how you were browsing in an antique store and found some hidden treasure, the preacher, functioning as narrator, asks, "Have you ever come across an unexpected find, a kind of hidden treasure? Maybe it was in an antique store or at a garage sale . . ." Buttrick declares, "There is *always* some other way of shaping an illustration so that we need not intrude on our own sermons."[5]

No doubt, Buttrick's advice on converting personal illustrations into the language of "common consciousness" is helpful in some circumstances, but not in *every* circumstance. Surely there is room in our preaching for a word of testimony, a word not about ourselves so much as about what God has been doing in our lives. There really is a difference between what a story is about and whom it happened to. The story may have happened *to you*, but that doesn't mean it's necessarily *about you*.

I think of all those stories Fred Craddock has told over the years, most of them personal stories, but almost none of them about himself.[6] Thomas Long refers to Craddock's approach as the "middle ground," neither the wholesale rejection of personal stories nor exclusive use of autobiography, but a healthy balance.[7] We don't really need a rule for whether to use personal illustrations or not. It's more like Winnie-the-Pooh's defense of some words Piglet didn't care for in one of Pooh's poems: "'They wanted to come in . . .' explained Pooh, 'so I let them. It is the best way to write poetry, letting things come.' 'Oh, I didn't know,' said Piglet."[8] Letting stories come, personal or otherwise, is sometimes the best way to write sermons.

Long suggests that if we do need a rule, the most important would be to monitor our intent. Temptations toward self-deprecation or hero worship are always subtle. Satan does not take preachers high upon the steeple of the church and dare them to throw in a personal anecdote so they might enter into glory. Hardly. We simply find ourselves tossing in a personal story to fill a hole in the sermon, and without much introspection. But while preachers may not always have their radars tuned to motives, Long notes that parishioners usually do. "Listeners are surprisingly savvy about discerning not only what we are saying about ourselves but also why we are saying it."[9]

Personal Reflection

What are your views on the use of personal illustrations? Do you use them? If so, how often do you use personal stories? Are they typically about you or more about something or someone you have encountered? What do you like about personal stories? What do you dislike? How could you examine your motives more closely with regards to autobiography in the sermon?

Scriptural Meditation

"The glory of the LORD has risen upon you." (Isaiah 60:1)

Painting with a Larger Palette

Remember those boxes of crayons with sixty-four colors—not the boxes with a measly eight or so, but the really big boxes? Those larger boxes have something to say to us preachers whose sermons are all too often limited in artistic flair, especially in the range of the illustrations we use. We know there are different kinds of illustrations from which to draw—pardon the pun—still, unless we are careful, we resort to the same kind time after time, a box of eight or even less. By *kind*, I refer not to content, stories from our glory days in high school sports or giving birth to children, but to the different types of illustrations. Let me explain.

Although this chapter refers to "brainstorming *stories*," it might be more helpful to think of illustrative material in three categories: analogy, story, and imagery.[10] Analogies, comparisons intended to make the point, are the most popular of the three. The preacher tells about a science experiment: if you place a frog in scalding water, it will jump out; but if you place it in lukewarm water and slowly raise the temperature, it will boil to death. You can see where it's going. It's an analogy, a comparison about the subtlety of temptations or some such application. And while this particular analogy has perhaps been overused and is a bit pedantic, not all analogies are. For instance, I read recently in a collection of essays the following lines:

> We [Americans] talk about our money the same way that Harvard students talk about their grades—in terms guarded, vague, and self-deprecating all at once. "How did you do on your paper?" "Oh, not so well—terribly, really." (One would later find that student's name on the short list for a Fulbright.) We won't say how much we have or make, but it certainly isn't enough.[11]

As the saying goes, "That'll preach!" It's an analogy. We're not preaching on GPAs at Ivy League schools, but the analogy works, especially on Stewardship Sunday. At least we hope it works.

Unfortunately, analogies have their drawbacks. Even a good analogy can distract listeners. It's possible, for instance, that someone could become more interested in grade inflation at Harvard and at least momentarily miss the emphasis on stewardship. Or imagine some junior high kids who decide to try a science experiment of their own one lazy Sunday afternoon. With eyebrows raised, one of them says to another, "Did you hear what the preacher said this morning about frogs?" Still, the main problem with analogies, helpful as they may be, is they are about something else—grades, frogs, and so forth—and if that "something else" is interesting—and why would we tell it if it's not?—listeners could be distracted. This is one of the major problems with so many children's sermons.[12]

Stories are different. Oh, sure, listeners can be distracted over any number of things in a story; but stories not only capture attention, they are about the subject at hand. Instead of comparisons with frogs and boiling water, the preacher tells about an actual case of someone slowly slipping into a destructive behavior—a spouse having an affair or a businessperson working the numbers. Or instead of comparing the grades of Harvard coeds to Americans' false modesty over wealth, maybe the preacher tells a story instead, like this one:

> Fred Craddock tells about taking part in a conference years ago at Clemson University where he was to lecture. Before he spoke a young woman got up to give a devotional thought on world hunger. He didn't know her. Mid-20s, soft voice. She had a legal-pad with her notes on it. He figured they were there for the night, one of those devotionals that drags on forever. Instead, she repeated one sentence over and over. She said the sentence in a foreign language, one Fred didn't know. Then she said it again in another language. Over and over, but each time in a different language. He lost count she said it so many times.
>
> When she said it in German he was pretty sure what it meant. In French, again he was pretty sure. When she said it in English, everybody knew. She said, "Mommy, I'm hungry." Then she sat down.
>
> Fred said he thought about that all the way back to Atlanta. And as he approached the city the first billboard he saw read, "All You Can Eat, $5.99." In his head he heard the woman's voice, "Mommy, I'm hungry."[13]

Even when their content is similar, analogies and stories are different. They simply work differently: the former a comparison to help listeners understand a concept, the latter a flesh-and-blood account of the concept itself. As skilled painters, we might even find a time to use both on the same canvas, within the same sermon, maybe even back-to-back.

The third type of illustration—images—though related to the first two, is noticeably different. Images are not full-blown stories, narratives with plot and characters. They are not identical with analogies, either. Images are picturesque, however, pictures for the imagination. And they can come from a variety of sources.

We might, for instance, be preaching a sermon or series of sermons on the church, its foibles and its hopes. In a sermon on Paul's many concerns for the divided church at Corinth, the preacher might ask the congregation to imagine a huge jigsaw puzzle in which the picture on the box is a snapshot of a church with members gathered round it holding hands. She might explain Paul's— and God's and her own—passionate desire to see the church put back together again, the way it was when the picture was taken.

Not all images are imagined. Some are rooted in observation and history. For example, Frederick Buechner uses architecture as inspiration when he notes how the vaulted ceiling of many a church sanctuary resembles the hull of a ship turned upside down—the nave, we call it. "Just about everything imaginable is aboard, the clean and the unclean both. . . . But even at its worst, there's at least one thing that makes it bearable within, and that is the storm without."[14] The church as ship, it's an image.

On occasion, an image might actually emerge from a story told, but take on a life of its own throughout the sermon, become a kind of controlling metaphor. Richard Lischer, for instance, in his widely read memoir *Open Secrets*, tells about the first church he served and how, as he arrived, one of the first things he noticed was the steeple "with a copper cross from which one arm was mysteriously missing."[15] It's an image.

One of the most overlooked sources for imagery is the biblical texts themselves. To cite just one example, Paul portrays baptism in terms of clothing, "As many of you as were baptized into Christ have clothed yourselves with Christ" (Galatians 3:27). What a graphic image for a sermon on the church as body of Christ! Gail

Ramshaw has identified forty different biblical images in the lectionary's cycle of readings—images such as body, light, shepherd, and water—along with helpful background information and ideas for preachers.[16] What a wonderful resource to remind us of the wealth of imagery right before us in the Scriptures!

Personal Reflection

What types of illustrations do you favor most in your preaching—analogy, story, imagery? Can you think of another type? What do you like about each? What do you dislike? Do you vary the types from time to time? What would you most like to change about the kinds of illustrations you tell?

Scriptural Meditation

"*People tell of your wondrous deeds.*" *(Psalm 75:1)*

Stocking the Well

For many of us, what we would most like to change about our illustrations is simply to find more of them, and good ones, too. We hear Barbara Brown Taylor preach and wonder where all those wonderful stories and images come from, where she finds them, how she remembers them when she needs them. Truth be told, we may even be jealous of her gifts and of preachers like her, which Julia Cameron claims is one sure sign we may be "creatively blocked" ourselves.[17] In actuality, the creativity we desire resides in us already. Recall the distinction between envy, desiring what we do not have, and jealousy, desiring what we already have but do not cherish.

I suspect Cameron is right when she notes elsewhere how the ideas we seek—the illustrations we so desperately need between now and Sunday—are there, waiting to be found, maybe even wanting to be found. According to one Hasidic rabbi, there is a constant outpouring from above that becomes apparent only when someone is there to receive it.[18] When it comes to preaching, I certainly believe that stories are gifts from God, who never withholds good things from us. "We have forgotten," writes Cameron, "that our creativity is a spiritual gift with its taproot in Spirit and not in our own will."[19] Often, we become hunters desperately seeking a story for this Sunday, rather than gatherers who have been collecting stories all along. Consider again Anne Lamott's wisdom that if your spouse locks you out of the house, your problem isn't with the door. "The word *block* suggests that you are constipated or stuck, when the truth is that you're empty."[20]

Perhaps the reason we can't find the right story when we need it is because the well has run dry. Stories go out from us, but perhaps not enough are coming in. The result? We become malnourished. We have demanded creativity and stories of ourselves but haven't properly nourished their source. I am thinking in particular of the lack of reading by preachers these days. I'm not thinking about online reading or skimming headlines. I'm talking about books. Fast food will not nourish us, not over time. And if our shelves are lined with only chicken soup, no wonder our souls are still hungry. Soup is mostly water, after all.

I know this to be the case because not that many years ago I was reading way too little myself. Oh, I read books in my field and the like, as well as the occasional spy novel, and published sermons by others, but I wasn't reading enough fiction, enough memoirs, enough essays. Although I gave credit where credit was due, I didn't read enough on my own, preferring instead to let others do the work for me.

I remember one desperate week coming across an essay in which Frederick Buechner cited Graham Greene's novel *The Power and the Glory* as one of the best ever written. He went on to quote a poignant passage from the book, a scene in which the renegade priest is dying without dignity. I loved the passage, and so, with Sunday coming, I used it. I supplied the context the best I could for not having read a single page of the novel, then shared the passage. It worked of course. Why wouldn't it? The only thing was I hadn't read the novel. I do not consider that omission a matter of ethics. I never pretended I'd read it. No, I consider it more a matter of survival, my soul being at stake. Sometime later I picked up a copy of the novel and devoured it. When I came to that passage, it came alive as never before. In that moment I knew the whisky priest personally, felt his struggles.

Where would we preachers be without the likes of John Steinbeck, Ernest Hemingway, and Chaim Potok, or more recently Gail Godwin, Barbara Kingsolver, Kathleen Norris, Annie Dillard, Alice Walker, Andre Dubus, and John Updike to name only a few writers? The list goes on and on. I still don't read as much as some preachers I know, but the reading I have done has made the difference between day and the proverbial dark night of the soul.

Personal Reflection

Are there times the well seems dry when it comes to finding stories? What do you do in those times? Was there a time in your life when you read more? What happened to cause the change? Do you miss forays into great literature? Is there something you've been intending to read for some time?

Scriptural Meditation

"So I took the little scroll from the hand of the angel and ate it."
(Revelation 10:10)

Renewal
The Sacrament of Reading

*"It looks like a book, but it is a world. A marvelous alchemy.
Or better, a transubstantiation, a sacrament."*
— Nancy M. Malone[21]

*"Why are we reading, if not in hope of beauty laid bare,
life heightened and its deepest mystery probed?"*
— Annie Dillard[22]

I grew up reading. Literally. Which is to say, reading helped me grow up. My earliest reading memories spring from Miss Simpson's first-grade class. I was in love not only with my teacher but with all those books in her room. As I recall, for each book read, we added a round-shaped piece of construction paper with our names on it to the ever-growing body of a dachshund—a "wiener dog" as we called them—that encircled the room just above the chalkboard. I was determined to win, to read the most books; and although my motives were not always pure, Miss Simpson instilled in me a love for reading. I spent countless hours with books, including a stash of Dr. Seuss titles in the bathroom at home, of all places. It wasn't until years later that I learned Martin Luther's Reformation ideas came in that same locale. I was in love with books!

The love waned at times. All loves do, but the admiration was constant. It was one of the many reasons I pursued a PhD. I figured another degree and a career in theological education would provide further opportunities for reading. I was right, although there were surprises. I can still remember the seminar my first semester in PhD studies, an introduction to scholarly life, including oral exams over Kate Turabian's *A Manual for Writers*, which the professor required us to memorize as if it were the Bible: "Anyone remember Turabian 3:16?"

In addition to Turabian, the only other book I remember as required for that course was *How to Read a Book*, by Mortimer J. Adler and Charles Van Doren. What an incredibly boring book! It reminds me of what Mark Twain once said about another title, "chloroform in print." Adler and Van Doren's book was/is considered a classic, a must for those wishing to sharpen their skills at what the authors call "intelligent reading." Trust me, it is deadly dull! To the authors' credit, the volume does include chapters on reading imaginative literature—poems, plays, and the like—but even those chapters are as dry as a Kansas wheat field.

As every seminary graduate can testify, the reading list for classes can often squeeze the opportunity for creative reading out of you like toothpaste from a tube. In some ways theological education for many of us helped to develop our "intelligent reading" skills, while simultaneously destroying our "creative reading" skills. What a shame! As a seminary professor, I should add in self-defense that some required reading will never be pleasurable, even though necessary. But that being said, a theological education ought also to make room for poetry and short stories. With that in mind, for the last few years, I've required students in the introductory homiletics course to read several short stories.

I was not surprised when a feature in the *Christian Century* revealed studies indicating that very few pastors read for pleasure. Or if they do, they don't admit it, which says something else entirely about us preachers. According to the study, Episcopal clergy read the most, right at five hours per week, in addition to sermon preparation. Five hours per week? That's the most? Even so, the study noted that most ministers, Protestant as well as Catholic, read books mainly about ministry. Only a select few admitted to reading fiction and memoirs, and some of those titles were suspect.[23] I'm recovering from that same affliction. I didn't always balance recreational and technical titles.

I suspect I'm not alone. "Hi, I'm Mike, and my reading habits are not what they should be." And a room of guilt-ridden ministers look awkwardly at the floor and respond, "Hi, Mike."

The truth is though, I *am* recovering. Maybe you are too. Sometimes I wonder if the recovery group I most need now is one for those addicted to books. I have become like Sara Nelson, who acknowledges there are "so many books, so little time," the title of her book about the adventures of reading.[24] She describes how true readers, when between books, become obsessed with the search for their next "read," their next literary adventure. Isn't that the truth? It's not so much that we pick out a book, she notes, but the book picks us out. To be addicted to books is to love the look of books, the smell of books, the joy of holding a really good one, even after it's over, savoring it. To be in love with reading is to enjoy even the simple pleasure of turning pages.

Honestly, I don't mean to sound like Chicken Little, "The literacy rates are falling!" but I worry about the reading habits of preachers these days. On many a Sunday I sit in pastors' studies—or is that "offices"?—scanning their libraries, most of the titles outdated and dusty. Or maybe some of the books they read for pleasure are kept at home, away from the scholarly stuff and the eyes of curious visitors. That separation, if indeed it exists, says something about our approach to preaching. Still, I wonder what has become of the love for reading.

Not surprisingly, Pulitzer prize–winning author Annie Dillard loved books at a young age. She compares the books of her childhood with bombs. Every title she picked up "was a land mine you wanted to go off," she writes. "You wanted it to blow your whole day. Unfortunately, hundreds of thousands of books were duds. They had been rusting out of everyone's way for so long that they no longer worked. There was no way to distinguish the duds from the live mines except to throw yourself at them headlong, one by one."[25]

"Read in order to live," wrote French novelist Gustave Flaubert, which is another way to call reading a sacrament.[26] We read not just to find stories for Sundays but to keep ourselves alive the other six days of the week—which, when taken together, eventually add up to a lifetime. Nancy Malone goes so far as to compare reading to a kind of contemplative prayer, in which "we're taken completely out of ourselves," only later to return refreshed.[27] That reminds me of the distinction sometimes made between the terms *prayers* and *prayer*.[28] Prayers, of course, are what we offer up to God in words. Prayers—plural—are what we say. Prayer—singular—is a way of life. Viewed this way, no wonder Malone compares reading to prayer. And no wonder so many of us are moved to worship God when reading a poignant piece of literature. The closing scene in *The Grapes of Wrath* comes to mind. Do you remember it?

Preacher Dates

— Reread a favorite book you haven't read in a while
— Buy a collection of short stories and dive into a different one each week for a month
— Read aloud to a child; borrow one if you have to
— Join a reading group, clergy-led or maybe not
— Pick one classic novel you've always promised yourself you would read someday
— Spend half a day in a bookstore browsing through titles until one of them finds you
— Ask a librarian or trusted friend for suggestions on a "good read"
— Read Ken Follett's *The Pillars of the Earth* (trust me!)
— Read a really good poem, and reread it slowly and often
— Find an ice cream or coffee shop and treat yourself while reading a favorite title

> *"This is how you read a novel: you inhale the experience.*
> *So start breathing."*
> —Azar Nafisi[29]

> *"You can't get a cup of tea large enough or*
> *a book long enough to suit me."*
> —C. S. Lewis

A Hundred Million Miracles

The musical genius Oscar Hammerstein wrote, "A hundred million miracles are happening every day."[30] All right, so maybe musicians are prone to exaggeration the way we ministers are. And even if the number is off—too high? too low?—epiphanies may be rare only because of our limited vision. Recall those two disciples shuffling back to Emmaus who finally recognize Jesus when he opens their eyes at a meal of broken bread. Recall Moses in the wilderness who turns aside to see a blazing shrub, and that line from Elizabeth Barrett Browning, about how every bush is on fire with God's presence, but only a few remove their sandals, while "The rest sit 'round it and pluck blackberries."[31] Or as the poet Mary Oliver observes, "This is the first, wildest, and wisest thing I know, that the soul exists, and that it is built entirely out of attentiveness."[32]

I suspect most of us have already encountered illustrations enough to last a lifetime of preaching; we just didn't pay close enough attention or write them down. Depressing, isn't it? One weekday afternoon a few years ago I ran across a fascinating title on the clearance table at a local bookseller: *Spiritual Literacy*, by Frederic and Mary Ann Brussat.[33] The book is the culmination of a project that a husband and wife team undertook when they were in seminary years ago, namely, cataloging epiphanies under a variety of headings: bread, washing dishes, candles, insects, seeds, and the like—yes, it has an index. They define spiritual literacy as "the ability to read the signs written in the texts of our own experiences."[34]

Like most people, preachers see movies, read the papers, go to concerts, and buy groceries. To us, however, is given the unique imperative to learn to look for signs of God's presence in those experiences. We must do so to stay alive, as should all people really; and we should do so as persons called to speak a word on God's behalf, come Sunday. If we are lucky, we will suffer from that disease writer Susan Sontag calls *Attention Surplus Disorder*. She says, "The easiest thing in the world for me is to pay attention."[35]

Preachers who keep daily journals have the advantage here. Not only do they take time to record thoughts on the day but many of them afford themselves time to record stories they have encountered in the process. I do not keep a journal myself, and while I have always filed away stories in one fashion or another, I have begun to record happenings in my life that might someday make a cameo appearance in a sermon. For instance, I remember boarding a flight out of Kansas City, where I live, and meeting a man with his Seeing Eye dog, a friendly German shepherd. The small talk eventually gave way to our careers. Turns out, he travels all across America speaking to gatherings of blind persons. He told me that most blind people never leave their homes. "Oh, sure," he said, "you see blind people on occasion, but there are many more who never go anywhere. They're afraid to go out and live." This fellow journeys with his dog to strange cities, makes his way on and off planes, catches taxis, and speaks on what it means to live courageously. I have never told this story in a sermon, but I might someday. At least I have it written down.

Of course, paying attention means attending to more than just our own lives. Ministers attend conferences at various times, and inevitably someone will tell a story worth remembering. And most ministers do remember it, the way most of us remember jokes we hear—for a day or two. Ministers listen to National Public Radio, with its many "driveway moments," stories so captivating we don't even get out of the car until they are finished. But how many of these same ministers write these things down?

Personal Reflection

How would you rank your ability to pay attention to life's little epiphanies? Think about some of the little happenings in your life this past week. What did they say to you? What do you think of keeping a journal of life's events? Do you record ideas for sermon illustrations? What story have you heard recently that impressed you? How do you plan to recall it when needed?

"Were not our hearts burning within us while he was talking to us on the road?" (Luke 24:32)

Being Kind to Gremlins

Ask any group of preachers where they get their stories, the sources for their illustrations, and the responses are likely to be newspapers, movies, books, other preachers' sermons, current events, personal life, Internet, . . . on the list goes. It's not only a predictable list; it's fairly useless. True, these are some of the most likely sources, but when it's time to find a story for Sunday, being reminded that movies are a source is not likely to help. Sure, newspapers are a source, but where's the perfect story we're looking for to help with this Sunday's sermon?

Brainstorming may be the key. But we have to understand what it means. Most of us have heard the advice about brainstorming, how essential it is keep an open mind, not become too critical or too selective too early in the process. If you want to brainstorm stories, say the experts, don't reject out of hand any idea that arises. This is good advice, but easier said than done. It's so hard in fact that one of my daughter's high school teachers distinguishes between brainstorming and brainpuking. Brainpuking, claims this teacher, is the process of letting *every* idea come out, not just a few, as with brainstorming. Not a pretty picture, but definitely good advice.

Don Wardlaw, who taught preaching at McCormick Theological Seminary, puts it another way—being kind to gremlins.[36] By gremlins he means the creative juices in all of us, the muses that reside within. He imagines them not so much in our brains as in our guts. Wardlaw says that when we begin to brainstorm ideas— stories or otherwise—the first gremlin comes to the surface with an idea. That's what gremlins do, especially the first one. If we reject the initial idea, "Nah, that won't work. What else do you have?" the gremlin goes back and says to the others, "Forget it, he's way too picky today." Or, "It's not worth it, she won't like anything we say." In other words, the gremlin factory shuts down. If, however, we respond, "Yeah, that's good. What else do you have?" the first gremlin reports to the others, "You won't believe this, she'll take anything today. Let's keep the ideas coming, fellows." And pretty soon the ideas are most definitely coming.

Anyone who has ever served on a committee that was assigned the task of brainstorming knows the truth of this approach. If some overbearing person keeps critiquing the ideas of others, pretty soon the ideas stop coming. Wardlaw says the same thing happens when it comes to brainstorming. So Sunday is coming, and we have done our exegetical work and decided on the sermon's focus. As we begin to search for stories, contemporary images and analogies for our message, we send word to the gremlins, "Keep the ideas coming! We are looking for stories! Keep them coming!"

Personal Reflection

During those times when the perfect story doesn't find you, how do you find stories for your sermons? How would you describe your relationship with the gremlins? Have they abandoned you? Have you neglected them?

"The fear of the LORD is the beginning of knowledge." (Proverbs 1:7)

Focus, Not Hocus-pocus

Contrary to popular opinion, there is nothing magical about finding stories. They are everywhere, even the elusive one we seek for this Sunday. No, not magic, but focus, is yet another key to finding stories. Let me explain. Imagine that I tell you I'm writing the great American novel. Like Snoopy, my first line reads, "It was a dark and stormy night . . ." I inform you that the story is set in medieval England, but that I'm stuck on what should happen next. So I ask for your opinion: "Any ideas? What do you think should happen next?" Of course, being a novel, the whole thing is a story, but it's impossible for you to say. You can brainstorm all you want; there is simply no way for you to suggest ideas when you haven't the foggiest notion what the novel is about.

The same goes for sermons and the search for stories. We look in vain for stories if we haven't a clear idea what kind of story we need. The novel is about medieval England; the sermon is about ancient Galilee. So what? It's not enough information. For instance, imagine that instead of my coming to you with the unfinished novel, you come to me with your sermon in progress. "I need a story for this sermon. Any ideas?" Ideas? Of course I have ideas for stories. I know a lot of stories. Everyone does. I could tell you about all the things that went wrong at my wedding. It was a disaster at the time, but it's funny now. It's a good story. Or I could tell you about a close encounter with a shark during my teen years of surfing on the Gulf coast. It's a really good story! Interested in either of those? You might be interested, but the point is obvious enough. We preachers don't look for "stories"; we look for *the perfect* story. And the search is made much easier when our focus is clear. What is the sermon about?

I have found that when I narrow the focus of the kind of story I'm looking for, the chances of finding such a story greatly increase. For instance, "I'm looking for a story about how the traditions we practice over a lifetime form us, how we are shaped by the rituals we enact." Simply finding a story is easy enough; it's like finding a generic box of cereal, yellow cover without the rooster on it, just the word "Flakes." We're not really looking for those kinds of stories, generic illustrations. Thus, we identify our focus in our search for stories.

Personal Reflection

How well defined is your sermon's focus when you seek stories? How successful was your story search for last week's sermon? Think about the sermon for this week. What kind of story do you need in relation to the sermon's focus?

Scriptural Meditation

"Gladden the soul of your servant." (Psalm 86:4)

Orality and Community

As we noted in the introduction, sermons most often are prepared in silence and isolation, even though they are always preached aloud and in community. This insight has something to say about our search for illustrative material. Brainstorming need not be an isolated activity, sequestered away in our monastic cell. Sermon preparation benefits not only from silence and prayer, but also from sounding out ideas with others.

With every sermon I prepare there comes a moment, sometimes more than one, when I knock on the door of David May, my New Testament colleague and good friend. I know, not everyone has the luxury of discussing sermon ideas with a biblical scholar; but the discussion is more often about possible stories than about exegetical issues. The scenario usually plays out in one of three ways. In every case it begins like this: "David, I'm stuck." "So what's new?" he asks. "Seriously, I'm looking for a story on how God is present in our lives not just in the big stuff—the life-changing epiphanies—but in the mundane moments as well. Any ideas?" Sometimes, amid the many ideas that occur to him, one of his suggestions fits. Mission accomplished. "Well done, thou good and faithful friend," I tell him. "I'll footnote you come Sunday."

Other times, the stories he suggests are not quite right but trigger a story in me that I had not thought of on my own. "Oh, that's good, but that reminds me of another story. Thanks. No footnote, but thanks." Still other times, he doesn't even say a word. "David, I'm stuck. I'm looking for a story on how God is present in our lives. . . . Oh, I've got it. Thanks." Not a word. How can that be? Not a word from David, but somehow hearing myself speak aloud triggers ideas. Orality, that's how. Speaking aloud is a powerful resource.

And so are the people with whom we sojourn. We could brainstorm ideas aloud even when alone, but colleagues contribute more than we might imagine. Lectionary groups will often do this. Many a preacher can testify to how helpful it is to sit down with other preachers and discuss ideas. Some preachers do the same with parishioners as well. At a midweek Bible study, for instance, the preacher will lead an informal discussion of the text to be preached this coming Sunday, inviting people to interact. Ministers who do this often find that not only do good ideas come for the sermon—stories, insights, applications—but the listeners come to church with a deeper level of anticipation and excitement for having been involved in the process of preparation.

Personal Reflection

Have you ever tried voicing aloud your search for an illustration? Who are the ministerial colleagues with whom you discuss sermon ideas? How does that group function? If you're not part of such a group, what do you think of the possibilities of starting your own or joining one already formed in your community? What are your reactions to leading a discussion/study of the text with the congregation ahead of Sunday?

Scriptural Meditation

> "Now the whole group of those who believed were of one heart." (Acts 4:32)

Renewal
The Sacrament of Friends

"I get by with a little help from my friends."
—John Lennon

"I do not call you servants any longer, . . . but I have called you friends."
—Jesus (John 15:15)

"Of all earthly realities," writes Nancy Malone, "more than bread and wine and oils and incense, human beings, body and soul, are sacraments of God, of God's presence."[37] Nowhere is this more borne out than in our friends. Friendship is a sacrament.

In Henri Nouwen's *Sabbatical Journey*, a diary of the year before he died, he writes extensively, among other things, about friendship. Even on the pages in which the entries are not about friends per se, it is his friends who impacted his sabbatical leave the most. On his entry for September 4, 1995, he tells about driving to Toronto to eat with his close friends Nathan and Sue. He writes, "When I think about the pains and joys of my life, they have little to do with success, money, career, country, or church, but everything to do with friendships." Over and over in his journal Nouwen tells about time with friends, watching a Paul McCartney concert on TV, taking Eucharist in a home, going out to eat—all of it with friends. The evening he spent with friends in Toronto, they watched the movie *Apollo 13*, with all of its tragedies and triumphs. Nouwen writes, "As the three of us watched it, I realized that somehow we too are astronauts in a spaceship trying to make it home safely. I guess that is true of all people who take the risk of friendship."[38]

What an interesting phrase, the "risk of friendship." I recall so many painful moments in my life when I had to say good-bye to friends—one of us moving away. That is part of the risk of friendship to be sure. No wonder so many Web sites promise to reunite us with old friends.

I am lucky. One of my two best friends lives only three hours away, and I see him more or less regularly, at golf gatherings and the like. My other best friend teaches New Testament at the seminary where I teach. His office is next door to mine. As Ralph Waldo Emerson wrote, "My friends have come unsought. The great God gave them to me."

Preacher Dates

— Call up a friend who lives close by and go to lunch together — better yet, dinner
— Call up a friend who lives out of town; calling is better than e-mail any day
— Plan a reunion with a group of friends you haven't seen in a while
— Take a friend to a ball game, or a favorite museum, or a movie
— Agree to read a book together; maybe John Irving's *A Prayer for Owen Meany*
— Buy a gift for a friend; better yet, make something yourself to give away

"My friends are my estate."
—Emily Dickinson

FIVE

⁓⊱⊰⁓

STAGE THREE: CREATING A SEQUENCE

"And now for my eighteenth, and, um, final point."

The Study Becomes Studio

Once when Robert Frost was reading some of his poems, he began to playfully chide the audience for not recognizing the meter, or tropes in general, or that a certain piece was synecdoche in particular. Gleefully he proclaimed, "I'm a synecdochist by profession." When he finished, a kind older lady who had become increasingly agitated during the whole ordeal, stood up and protested, "But Mr. Frost, *surely* when you are writing one of your *beautiful poems*, *surely* you can't be thinking about *technical tricks*!" She spat out those last words as if they were bile. Frost leaned into the microphone, and with the grin of the Cheshire cat, exclaimed, "I revel in 'em."[1]

The move from stage one to stage two involves a certain degree of creativity, to be sure, but the transition to this third stage demands even more. It is here, in creating a sequence, that we revel in the "technical tricks" of preaching. Here, the pastor's study is transformed into a studio. Here, the preacher as scholar becomes preacher as artist, too.

H. W. Janson, in his monumental *History of Art*, distinguishes between merely *making* and *creating*. The former, he says, is more of a craft, like the making of candles for example. There are rules to be followed: when to add the dye and scent, the proper temperature of the wax at pouring, cooling the mold, and so forth. Creating, in contrast, is less precise and much more imaginative, and Janson invites readers to consider Pablo Picasso's bronze cast entitled *Bull's Head* as an example.

Janson notes, "The handiwork—the mounting of the seat on the handlebars—is ridiculously simple. What is far from simple is the leap of imagination by which Picasso recognized a bull's head in these unlikely objects."[2] Creating, then, is not creating from scratch. Picasso did not invent the bicycle, or the bull's head, for that matter. And fortunately we do not invent the sermon. No, creating is the imaginative act of putting things together. "Though we cannot create matter," wrote theologian and mystery writer Dorothy Sayers, "we continually, by rearrangement, create new and unique entities."[3] In the case of preaching, we are given the creative task of arranging the biblical material—as unearthed in stage one—and contemporary material—as brainstormed in stage two—that will make up the sermon. In so doing we seek to become cocreators with the creative God, whose speaking always seeks to create anew.

Believe it or not, though, the crafting of a sermon is a touchy subject with teachers of preaching, many of whom debate just what part preachers play in the process—the role of rhetoric. The particulars of the debate date back to the late fourth, early fifth century, when the rhetorically trained Aurelius Augustine was converted to Christianity. He brought with him not only his shady past but his rhetorical training as well. At the time there were church leaders who considered the study of rhetoric itself as shady, something demonic, for which preachers would be held accountable before God in the final judgment.[4] Not everyone of course held such fanatical views, but rhetoric was definitely suspect by many in the church.

Augustine was of a different persuasion. Largely influenced by Cicero, Augustine wondered why eloquence should be a tool used only by those speaking falsehood and not by Christian preachers, an approach he laid out in what is considered the first homiletics textbook in the history of the church.[5] Today some teachers of preaching value rhetoric's role in preaching, at least to a degree, while others lament how rhetoric has often overshadowed the heavier theological issues of preaching.[6] That being said, every preacher makes rhetorical decisions when putting sermons together. Deciding what to say, how to say it, and in what order—all of these matters are rhetorical ones.

Cicero himself named five canons—or rules—of rhetoric for speakers, the second of which was arrangement.[7] After deciding what to say, claimed Cicero, speakers must next decide on the order in which to say it. Of course, preachers do this every week, much of it out of habit more than consciously. "Oh, I almost always begin with a joke or something humorous." "I prefer to close with a touching story." "Most weeks I like to summarize my key points near the end." "My favorite introduction is to explain the background of the scriptural text." "I generally prefer to follow a teaching moment in the sermon with some kind of illustration."

What is perhaps most alarming about these statements is not the rhetoric implied but the routine, which can be deadly dull from a rhetorical standpoint. In a fascinating article on imagination, Martin Marty contrasts the multiple moves in a game of chess with the predictability of so much preaching these days. Citing a book review from the *Times Literary Supplement*, he writes:

> The *Oxford [Chess] Companion* lists 701 chess openings or main variants on these openings. . . . There are 400 different possible positions after each player has made one move; 71, 852 after the second; once three moves have been made by white and black, the possible legal configurations exceed nine million. The number of distinct, non-repeating 40-move chess games which can be played is much greater than the estimated number of electrons in our universe.

Marty then describes how so many preachers with so many possibilities before them—different texts and stories, different images and metaphors, different occasions and so forth—get up week after week and drone, "The text for our morning meditation is written in the eleventh chapter of . . ." Marty writes, "And the congregation nods, knows it will nod, knows that nodding is expected of it, knows that the preacher knows that nodding is part of the transaction. Why? There is no imagination."[8] Our sermons become like a CD we've heard way too many times; we know the next track before it even starts. Predictable.

Personal Reflection

How do you normally begin your sermons? How do you normally end? How do you structure the message overall? What do you like about that pattern? What do you dislike? Was there a time when you arranged your sermons differently? Can you imagine a way other than your current pattern? How do you plan to arrange this week's sermon?

Scriptural Meditation

"Be gracious to me, O Lord." (Psalm 86:3)

_____

_____

_____

_____

_____

_____

_____

_____

_____

_____

Preaching outside the Box

Many busy preachers—which is of course the only kind—feel boxed in by the familiar, but then again we are often too busy to stop and do anything about it. We may be tired of the same old territory week in and week out, but at least it's familiar territory. We entertain notions of driving a different route from home to church, of letting go and enjoying life more, but before we know it, another day has come and the routine wins out. On rare occasions—maybe after attending a workshop on creative preaching—we entertain notions of trying a different style of preaching, but before we know it, another Sunday has come, and the sermon sounds like most every other sermon we've ever preached. And the truth be told, the same way it's possible to drive a familiar route in a daze is how we preach some weeks.

In his classic work *The Homiletical Plot*, Eugene Lowry includes a wonderful little puzzle for preachers.[9] You may have seen it elsewhere. The puzzle consists of nine dots arranged in three rows and three columns. The task is to connect all the dots without lifting your pencil off the page. The line must be straight with the exception of three turns. Here's the puzzle for you to try:

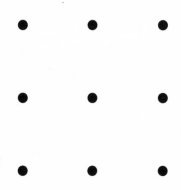

The solution often eludes people because they imagine they must stay within the confines of a box, when in truth no such box even exists. The mind imagines a box with borders. The solution imagines another way:

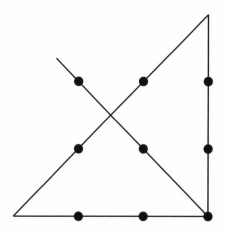

We preachers imagine our own boxes when it comes to shaping sermons. Confined by a lack of imagination or having been exposed to only one way of preaching in our upbringing and training—the stereotypical three points is perhaps the most common—we have trouble imagining a sermon outside the box. I speak from personal experience here.

As I shared before, I preached my first sermon before attending seminary. In fact, I preached probably half a dozen times before I ever took a course in preaching. Looking back I cringe at my attempts, although there was one thing about my preaching I did fairly well. Namely, the structure was anything but predictable. I knew nothing of outlining sermons. I had no idea how preachers came up with points, three or otherwise. I couldn't find any points in my Bible, not even in the margins. So I did what came natural to me. Sometimes I simply walked through the text, explaining and illustrating concepts that I eventually tried to apply to our situation. Other times I imported a metaphorical structure, such as the time when I asked listeners what their SQ was, their service quotient. Although the sermon's content was mine, I borrowed the idea for the sermon's form from another preacher I had heard. The sermon's structure came from a series of questions related to how we view serving others. There may have been three questions, maybe four. Before I went to seminary the structure of my sermons was anything but predictable. I enjoyed some sense of freedom early in my preaching ministry.

When I began my homiletical training, however, I learned how to outline sermons. Turns out, the process was not all that hard, resulting from a linguistic study of the text. If the Greek structure of a Pauline passage, for instance, conveyed three main ideas—as opposed to minor ones, subordinate clauses and the like—then the sermon's outline consisted of three main points. Amazing how often my read of Paul and others resulted in three points!

More amazing, however, was how over time I got to the point where I could see points everywhere. It wasn't until my doctoral studies in homiletics that I learned other ways—inductive and narrative, for instance. Our role models, our seminary training, our experimenting with our own way—all of these can, over time, lead to our falling into a rut, a stifling of creativity. The variety of the text's own structure can often be freeing.

I remember reading in one of those complimentary airline magazines an article about creativity. The author told how public schools and peer pressure in adolescent years often squeeze out of children the creativity and free thinking that came so naturally in younger years. For instance, the grade-school teacher asks the children to draw a tree. "Draw a picture of a tree, boys and girls." Little hands reach for a crayon and begin to outline a tree, which is then canopied with a leafy shape over the top.

Look familiar? It should. It's how most adults draw a tree as well, even though there's not a tree in the world that looks like that! Oh, on rare occasions one child in twenty will draw a tree in winter, its intricate branches exposed and intertwined. On even rarer occasions a child will reach for a rainbow of colors—reds and yellows, shades of gold—and draw her impressionistic remembrances of the sun filtering down through fall leaves.

The use of the feminine pronoun is intentional. In my experience women preachers evidence more creativity than men when it comes to shaping sermons. Maybe it's the lack of tradition-bound role models, maybe it's part of the feminine mystique. Who knows? For most of us, however, all our sermons look like all those trees we drew in kindergarten. Predictable.

Personal Reflection

If you were asked to draw a tree, what would yours look like? If you were asked to "draw a sermon," what would yours look like? What cultural influences do you remember as draining your creativity? How might the inner child in you find ways to partner with the preacher in you?

Scriptural Meditation

"Whoever does not receive the kingdom of God as a little child will never enter it." (Luke 18:17)

Putting a Puzzle Together

Ask most anyone how they go about putting a jigsaw puzzle together, and the answers are amazingly predictable. Most of us search out the four corners and all the straight pieces. Maybe a few rebels look for middle sections that are easily identified by a pattern of color, but most of us go about putting puzzles together in remarkably predictable fashion. It's the way our parents taught us and the way we taught our kids. And, by George, it works!

Of course, before we look for any of the pieces, corners or otherwise, we look at the picture on the box. We prop the cover of the box against the coffee table or the basket of fruit on the kitchen table. It is the picture on the cover that will guide our puzzle-solving adventure. Is there any other way? Well, sure, but it would drive most of us crazy. I mean we could turn the pieces upside down before us and proceed to put the puzzle together by determining which pieces fit together, without the benefit of the picture.

Crazy as that sounds, that is something of what confronts us when we put our sermons together. Arranging the pieces of the sermon is an open-ended enterprise. There is no picture to guide the process. Within reason we are free to arrange the sermon in any number of ways. The Bible says to preach, but it never says how to preach. Such news is liberating and frightening at the same time. Restraints may be restraining, but they are also familiar. If sermons can take any number of forms, how then shall we decide? What are some of the options we may never have considered?

For the most part, arrangement can be divided into two broad categories: *logical* and *experiential*. In logical sermon arrangement, the more traditional of the two, the preacher decides on the order of materials in the sermon's flow or argument. This type of arrangement views the sermon more as a study or presentation of material. For instance, the preacher wishes to posit two arguments for why stewardship of the earth's resources is crucial. One of the arguments is more convincing than the other. Which one should come first? Which will come last? Rhetorical studies refer to these concerns as issues of primacy and recency. A case can be made for our best point coming first, just as it can for our best point coming last. Logical arrangement is primarily about sequencing that appeals to the intellect of listeners.

Experiential arrangement is a relatively new phenomenon in preaching. Since the early 1970s, teachers of preaching have been stressing how sermons can be less like a Bible study or lecture and more of an event in which something happens. Rather than building a logical case for stewardship, the preacher evokes an image — or series of images — of what stewardship looks like in the flesh, much as we considered with stories in "Stage Two: Brainstorming Stories." Experiential arrangement entails sequencing a narrative adventure that listeners will experience in the hearing of the sermon.

In some ways these two patterns of sermon arrangement correspond to what French philosopher Henri Bergson referred to as different types of order: *geometric* and *living*. The first is orderly in the way a person's desk could be described as orderly, folders neatly stacked and so forth. The second is orderly in the sense that it represents life the way most of us would recognize it, not neat but most definitely recognizable.[10] Logical and experiential arrangement are different ways of putting sermons together.

Personal Reflection

Since not every preacher conceives of sermon preparation as an artistic enterprise, which type of arrangement best describes your style? Logical (geometric)? Experiential (living)? What aspects of the other type of arrangement interest you? What specifically?

Scriptural Meditation

  "See, I am making all things new." (Revelation 21:5)

Renewal
The Sacrament of Playing

"I arise in the morning torn between a desire to improve the world and a desire to enjoy the world. This makes it hard to plan the day."
—E. B. White

"On the day of judgment God will ask only one question: Did you enjoy my world?"
—Traditional Jewish saying

Harry S. Truman liked to play. Not just as a boy, eating striped candy with his granddad at the fair, but even as an adult. Truman liked to bowl with friends, and he loved to play cards. He was playing cards when he learned that FDR had died. Even in Truman's own last days, with his health failing, he and his good friend Thomas Melton, pastor of the First Presbyterian Church in Independence, Missouri, would set out regularly on a short walk. Truman did most of the talking, but not just with Melton. The former president developed an interesting ritual of stopping along the way at a certain gingko tree, a huge and majestic tree. Every time they walked, Truman would stop and say something to the tree, the same thing every time, "You're doing a good job."[11] What a fun story, and what a wonderful spirit of play!

Like Truman, most of us love to play, myself included. I enjoy everything from a round of golf to a friendly—OK, sometimes competitive—game of "H-O-R-S-E" in the driveway, from riding my daughter's electric-powered scooter around our cul-de-sac to a summer swim and a game of "Marco Polo." Everybody knows that playing is fun; it's just that some of us no longer *know* it in the biblical sense of the word. As a result, aging brings with it a stiffness of not only our joints but our spirits, too.

In his book *How to Think like Leonardo da Vinci*, Michael Gelb tells how frustrated church officials were with the artist's slow pace while he was working on his masterpiece *The Last Supper*. It seems da Vinci would often spend half a day or more just daydreaming, while the officials thought he should work at the same pace as those laboring in the fields. When confronted, da Vinci replied, "The greatest geniuses sometimes accomplish more when they work less."[12] Gelb strongly suggests readers not share that sentiment with their bosses in the corporate world, and I would agree when it comes to church boards and the like, but da Vinci's response reminds us that life consists of more than work, even church work. When do we play?

Consider the wisdom of G. K. Chesterton, the kind of person who obviously would have been fun to be with. He wrote in one of his notebooks:

> You say grace before meals.
> All right.
> But I say grace before the play and the opera,
> And grace before the concert and the pantomime,
> And grace before I open a book,
> And grace before sketching, painting,
> Swimming, fencing, boxing, walking, playing, dancing;
> And grace before I dip the pen in the ink.[13]

This is sacramental theology at its most sublime, recognizing the holiness of even playful moments. Saying grace before a swim? Before the opera? Before signing up for those tango lessons we've always craved? What a wild and wonderful worldview!

Chesterton's words remind me of Mary Cartledgehayes's inspiring memoir *Grace*. A preacher with all the struggles any minister encounters, she shares how when she and her husband discovered he was dying of cancer, they decided to savor every moment left, including her decision that they would have sex every day until he died. She writes:

> To breathe, to laugh, to curse, to praise, to weep, to sit in the midst of perfect order, to stand in the center of perfect chaos, to break bread, to eat three strawberries, to touch a piano's keys, to kiss a lover's skin, to birth, to baptize, to bless, to bury, to live, to die—either it is all holy, or none of it is holy.

Then she adds what just so happen to be the very last words of her book, "And this is what I know. It is all holy."[14]

— Play at a hobby you've always promised yourself, even something like boat building
— Play with the restoration of an antique, maybe even an antique car
— Play some tennis with a friend or hit the ball off a wall
— Play poker with some friends (gambling with pennies is optional)
— Play dominoes with those parishioners who've been inviting you for years
— Play in the rain with neighborhood kids
— Play some board games you love or some new ones that sound interesting
— Play hooky and enjoy a day with someone you love, maybe even yourself

> *"Most middle-class Americans tend to worship their work,*
> *to work at their play, and to play at their worship. . . .*
> *Their life-styles resemble a cast of characters in search of a plot."*
> —Gordon Dahl

> *"It is better to have a broken bone than a broken spirit."*
> —Lady Allen of Hurtwood[15]

Turning the Sermon Upside Down

The name Fred Craddock has become synonymous with inductive preaching since the 1971 publication of his revolutionary book *As One without Authority*.[16] At a time when some theologians were proclaiming the "death of God" and the futility of preaching, Craddock sounded a note of hope in favor of preaching. Drawing upon then recent trends in literary criticism of the Bible and developments in education theory, Craddock espoused a kind of preaching that turned the homiletical wisdom of the time on its head—figuratively and literally. Figuratively, he turned preaching theory on its head as he challenged long-held notions of what it means to preach.

Literally, he turned preaching upside down. Let me explain. Traditional preaching is deductive in nature. The sermon begins with a general statement of truth and then looks at the specific ramifications of that truth. In other words, the sermon begins with a general thesis—"In this passage the apostle Paul challenges our notion of freedom without constraints. This morning, then, let's consider what it means to live responsibly within the freedoms we have in Christ . . ."—and then spends the rest of the time expounding on what has already been clearly stated. Deductive preaching is most often diagramed like this:

In some ways, deductive preaching can be understood via an analogy with the old detective shows on television, like *Columbo*. Even if you've never seen the show, it's the same formula for any number of lawyer/detective shows of generations gone by. The opening scene is a murder to which we are privy as viewers. We know "whodunit" right from the start. For the next fifty minutes or so viewers watch as the detective tries to figure out what we already know. There is no suspense.

That lack of suspense describes deductive preaching in a nutshell. Very early on in the sermon listeners know what the sermon will be about, not the "whodunit" but the "what's-it-about." For the next so many minutes, hopefully less than fifty, the preacher will proceed down a line of thinking already made obvious in the earliest moments. Rhetorically, such predictability can be deadly, and we might be tempted to write it off altogether, but deductive arrangement doesn't have to be dull. Predictability, when accompanied with clarity, can be quite effective at conveying information. If we wish to say something to the church about the upcoming selection of elders who will serve the congregation, clarity and predictability are admirable qualities, and deductive patterns of logical arrangement work quite well. As Cleo LaRue, one of the leading African American homileticians, rightly notes, in the black church deductive preaching continues to be a powerful force.[17]

But what if the text is a parable of Jesus, one of those riddles Jesus told that leaves "the mind in sufficient doubt about its precise application," and thus teases listeners, as C. H. Dodd so aptly described it?[18] What then? That was one of Fred Craddock's many questions as a New Testament scholar.[19] His solution was inductive preaching, a turning of deductive preaching upside down, usually diagramed like this:

To understand inductive arrangement, you simply need to consider the newer lawyer/detective shows. Whether it's *Law and Order* or *CSI*, the formula goes something like this. The show starts with a murder. As viewers, we are not privy to the killer's identity.

There are clues, of course, or else we wouldn't watch. For the next fifty minutes or so, we, along with the stars of the show, will try to figure out "whodunit." It will come clear, of course, but not right away. Disclosure is part of the process itself.

This is something of how inductive preaching operates. Listeners know the text and are keenly aware of the bind—an essential in the plot of all good stories—but they don't know exactly where this sermon is taking them. There are clues along the way, or else they would tune out. There will be resolution near the end, or else they will be frustrated. But from the start there is an enigma with which to wrestle, a journey to be undertaken.

Generally speaking, inductive preaching relies upon two strategies for effect: questions and doubt. Neither of these come naturally to preachers. Or maybe they come *naturally*, but not *habitually*, to most preachers. Church members see their ministers as answer people, not question people. Over time, ministers come to see themselves the same way. Personally, I've never walked down the hall while Sunday morning Bible study classes were going on and had someone call me in with, "Hey, Mike, we were wondering if you could ask us a hard question about the Bible?" That's not how the scene goes, is it? Hardly. Instead, well-meaning church members ask us the questions, "So, preacher, what do you think Jesus really meant when he said . . . ?"

Inductive preaching turns that practice on its head. Inductive preaching invites listeners to ponder questions we preachers throw out for consideration. Instead of taking to the pulpit with declarative sentences, "The Bible calls us to be stewards of the earth's resources . . . ," we might ask:

> So why is care for the earth all that important anyway? I mean, seriously, in the big scheme of things aren't there weightier matters for Christians to consider? Doesn't the Bible have more to say about personal salvation than saving the earth?

Such questions are asked in sincerity, giving voice to the questions listeners have asked themselves from time to time. It's obvious enough we will answer the questions to some degree, just as it is obvious the detective will solve the murder case. Still, there is something compelling about a sermon that invites listeners to participate actively rather than be passive receptacles. As Fred Craddock so aptly put it, with traditional deductive preaching, if the listeners are a part of the team, "it is as javelin catcher."[20]

Inductive preaching also involves listeners by means of doubt, that rarest of commodities in Christian pulpits, even though it is commonplace in the hearts and minds of believers everywhere, even the hearts and minds of the preachers. The use of doubt is more than a foil, a sham used to dupe folks into listening. The inductive preacher gives voice to the doubts of us all. Instead of pronouncing, "The apostle Paul emphatically declares that all things work for good . . . ," we might do better to start the sermon like this:

> So Paul declares that all things work for good for those who love God. I'm not so sure. Oh, it's in the Bible and all, but do *all* things work for good? *All* things? If you believe that, then print those words on some business cards and take a stack with you everywhere you go. Take them to the oncology wing of the hospital. Pull one of the cards out of your pocket while watching the evening news or reading the local paper. Do you really think *all* things work together for good? Maybe Paul was expressing some wishful thinking on his part, or some future view of how things will be someday . . .

In the end, of course, the doubts expressed will give way to proclamation, much the way the detectives will catch the bad guys and so forth. The real world, however, unlike Hollywood's formulaic approaches, is not always so neatly wrapped up, so even our proclamations will have to acknowledge the complexities of our world. But doubt is such a fine way of getting into the sermon's subject matter.

Personal Reflection

Since most ministers were trained to do Bible study inductively and yet preach deductively, what are your reactions to inductive preaching? What are your initial impressions? How do the concepts of questions and doubts sound to you? How do you think your parishioners would respond to inductive preaching?

Scriptural Meditation

  "For who has known the mind of the Lord?" (Romans 11:34)

The Plot Thickens

If Fred Craddock's name has become synonymous with inductive preaching, then without question Eugene Lowry holds a similar status in the area of narrative preaching. He didn't invent the approach, any more than Craddock invented inductive preaching. In fact, in 1971, when Craddock asked why so many of our sermons sound the same, when the Bible is so diverse in style, it was Eugene Lowry and others who looked to the parables of Jesus — and the evangelists — for inspiration.

Drawing on the narrative nature of Scripture in general, the parables in particular, and the psychology of how plot works, Lowry popularized narrative preaching. His 1980 classic, *The Homiletical Plot*, took the Craddock revolution to the next stage.[21] Lowry's understanding of narrative is not so much about storytelling per se—sermons chock-full of one story after another—but rather about sermons with an overarching narrative feel. In other words, the sermon's flow moves from conflict, that essential in all stories, detective or biblical, to eventual resolution—in Lowry's case, one found in the good news of what God has done in Christ.[22]

Narrative preaching, like its cousin inductive preaching, has its strategies too. Allow me to name two primary ones, in addition to inductive tension: imagination and narration. Typically one component of a narrative sermon is retelling the story of the biblical text itself. Such a retelling could come early in the sermon or late; it could be interwoven throughout the flow, but a retelling will most likely constitute an important part of the narrative sermon.[23] That retelling will inevitably be enhanced by the use of imagination.

Imagination is such a wonderful word. Look it up in any dictionary; better yet, discover it for yourself in the pages of *Alice's Adventures in Wonderland* by Lewis Carroll or in J. K. Rowling's *Harry Potter* books. Imagination is what keeps us reading. It's what takes us back to the movies. It's what we love about children. Imagination truly is a wonderful word, but not with all preachers. Some preachers I know break out in hives when they hear that word. Or as biblical scholar Christopher Rowland suggests, "When it comes to the imagination, we are like people who, having had little exercise, find themselves severely taxed by strenuous physical effort. Our imaginations are out of condition."[24]

Even traditional preachers, however, use imagination to some degree. For instance, if the text is Luke's story about the woman who puts in two small coins during temple worship (Luke 21:1–4), most expository preachers include an explanation of the temple courtyard, the kind of coins she gave, and the like. So what, then, do I mean by the creative use of imagination in narrative preaching?

Narrative preaching seeks to incorporate the sermon's teaching moments narratively, in the retelling of the story itself. Narrative preaching, then, entails the use of imagination, but not an imagination run wild. Narrative imagination means fleshing out details of the text that are consistent with our study of the passage, but doing so in a more natural and narrative way. We don't interject, "Allow me to remind you for a moment as to what the temple courtyard in first-century Judaism would have looked like." Neither do we create fanciful details off the top of our heads, "Now, I just imagine that when she dropped those coins in the offering that day, she had made up her mind that . . ." Literary license is one thing—"This woman had run out of checks long before she ran out of deposit slips. There was nothing left in her account. This was the last of her resources"—but imagination gone amok is not what we seek.

Take, for example, another story in Luke, the bent woman whom Jesus restores (Luke 13:10–17). The story takes place in the synagogue on a Sabbath. A background study of synagogue worship reveals that the floors of ancient synagogues typically consisted of a mosaic of some sort. We also know that the menorah would have been present, as well as Torah scrolls. Being unable to stand upright, this woman could see the floor but not the menorah. She could pray but not in the customary Jewish posture of arms raised toward heaven. These are the kinds of imaginative details that could be fleshed out narratively in the sermon.

Narration is the other strategy for narrative preaching. That seems obvious enough, except that narration is amazingly simple and sophisticated at the same time. The simple part dates back to some of our earliest childhood memories, parents or grandparents telling us a story:

> Once upon a time there were three little pigs who left home. Each pig decided to build a house to protect him from the big bad wolf. The first pig was foolish and said, "I will build my house of straw." When the wolf came, he huffed and he puffed, and he blew down that pig's house. The second pig was foolish, too. He said, "I will build my house out of sticks."

It's familiar enough, the plot and all. But notice how the story is told, the variety of voices at work. The storyteller begins with the voice of narration: "Once upon a time there were three little pigs . . ." But the storyteller does more than just *tell* the story; comments are offered on how to *understand* the story: "The first pig was foolish . . ." Moments later, however, we hear another voice, that of the *character*: "I will build my house of straw." Sometimes the narrator is telling the story, sometimes commenting on it, other times allowing the characters to speak their own lines.

Strange as it may seem, these are the voices of narrative preaching as well: narrator, preacher, and characters.[25] There are portions of the narrative sermon in which we tell the story as narrator: "So Zaccheus lodged himself in a sycamore tree as Jesus and his followers approached the town of Jericho." There are other portions in which as preacher we help listeners to appreciate important aspects of the story as preacher: "Zaccheus wasn't just a tax collector, despised by his fellow Jews; he was a *chief* tax collector. This is the only chief tax collector mentioned in Scripture. The man was filthy rich, literally. Luke has much to say about possessions in his Gospel." Then at other times we allow the characters in the story to speak, demonstrating what our English teachers told us was the difference between indirect and direct discourse in good writing: " 'Today, I give half of my possessions to feed the poor . . .' "

Personal Reflection

What are your initial impressions of the word *imagination*? Do you consider yourself an imaginative person? An imaginative preacher? How do you normally employ imagination in your sermons? What are your reactions to a disciplined use of imagination in narrative preaching? Can you see how it's possible to both tell the biblical story and share insights into it? What part of narrative preaching intrigues you the most? What part scares you the most?

Scriptural Meditation

"Blessed are the pure in heart, for they will see God." (Matthew 5:8)

A Homiletical Slide Show

While inductive and narrative preaching are cousins, more and more teachers of preaching are embracing the term "episodic preaching" to encompass them both.[26] Episodic preaching entails viewing the sermon as a series of vignettes, stitched together in quiltlike fashion. Think of it as putting together a slide show. You can imagine a PowerPoint presentation if you want, although an old-fashioned carousel of slides will do just fine. Instead of conceiving of the sermon as so many major points—three, or a creative variation of two or four—the sermon consists of a series of slides. Some of them are exegetical in nature; others are illustrative; still others, some kind of application. These are the three areas—or boxes—out of which the sermon's possible slides will come. The total number of slides depends on the preacher. Instead of a three-point sermon of eight minutes each, for example, David Buttrick asks us to imagine a sermon with, say, eight segments lasting three minutes each.[27] That's something of the idea of episodic preaching.

As we have noted, the end of our textual study is the beginning of our sermon preparation, so to speak. In other words, sermons include not only textual/theological matters but contemporary analogies and stories as well. These two areas of material constitute the "stuff" of preaching. The preacher must decide not only what stuff will be included in—or excluded from—the sermon but also in what order it will occur. This is the very heart of creating a sequence.

One helpful way to move toward the creation of the sermon's sequence is to divide the possible material into two categories: *textual/theological* and *today*. On a piece of paper divided into two columns, I write the textual/theological material in the left-hand column. In the right-hand column I list some of the possible contemporary stories and images. For example, in a sermon I preached from Matthew 28:16–20, the two columns of possible material looked like this, although typically in a handwriting no one could possibly read:

Textual/Theological	Today
mountains in Matthew ("the" mountain)	my testimony — Terri's witness
baptizing and discipling as church's mission	recent conference speaker who gave us an offering
Christ's promise to be with them (Emmanuel)	tracing church history backwards from this mountain in Matthew
Matthew's changing of Mark's ending	writer's block — How would you end a Gospel?
appearance here in Gentile territory	Chloe Breyer's story of missionary in China
earlier mission to Jews only, now enlarged	Anne Lamott's conversion story
other places in Matthew where Jesus speaks — now his followers will	stories of seminarians and their calls — all started on this mountain

In theory, the sermon is now before us — only in the same way that a completed puzzle is before us shortly after we've dumped all the pieces on the coffee table. There is still a lot of work to be done. As we noted above, some preachers instinctively or habitually arrange their materials, and without much conscious reflection on the matter.

Personal Reflection

What are your impressions of episodic sermon flow? Does the freedom to arrange the slides excite you? How does that freedom scare you?

Scriptural Meditation

"Come to me, all you that are weary and are carrying heavy burdens." (Matthew 11:28)

_____

_____

_____

_____

_____

_____

_____

_____

_____

_____

_____

Drawing a Map

If someone in need of directions were to ask you to draw him a map, the first question you would ask is obvious: "To where?" Where exactly are you wanting to go? That's *destination*. It makes a difference if someone is trying to get to Fayetteville, Arkansas, as opposed to Toronto, Canada. In sermon mapping, the preacher starts with the sermon's destination, where we are trying to go—the sermon's focus, in other words. For that reason, Fred Craddock suggests that the preacher write the sermon's focus at the bottom of the two columns, not the top. Why? Because that's where the sermon is headed, not where it will start.

"What should come last?" is a key question as we begin to create a sequence. Sociologist Barry Schwartz notes that what comes last is frequently most influential in a person's experience of an event. In a laboratory study, people were asked to listen to two different soundtracks. The first consisted of an obnoxious sound lasting eight seconds, the second track included the same obnoxious eight seconds followed by eight seconds of slightly less obnoxious sound. When asked which they would prefer to hear again, the overwhelming majority selected the latter, despite the sound lasting twice as long. Why? Schwartz concludes, "Because whereas both noises were unpleasant and had the same aversive peak, the second has a less unpleasant end, and so was remembered as less annoying than the first."[28]

None of us wants to think of our sermons as annoying or obnoxious, but the evidence is clear that what comes last impacts listeners in powerful ways. The last slide in our show is not only what comes last in the sermon, not only what people will leave with, but where the sermon is headed. What comes last? is the first question.

The other obvious question when asked to draw someone a map is "Where will you be coming from?" That's *origination*. A map to Fayetteville, Arkansas, will not be the same if folks are coming from Little Rock, as opposed to Detroit, Michigan. Sermon mapping starts with the sermon's ending, but the next question is the sermon's opening. "What should come first?" The first moments of the sermon are crucial, as almost every preacher knows full well.

The destination and origination of the sermon can be found in either column — textual/theological or today. The sermon might open with a contemporary vignette: "Did you see that story in the newspaper the other day about . . . ?" Or it might begin with a textual insight: "Now why would Jesus make a dishonest steward the hero of his parable here in . . . ?" The same for the sermon's last slide; it can come from the biblical world or the contemporary world. My own preference is to use my most powerful slide nearer the end of the sermon. By powerful, I mean rhetorically impacting. It's not a hard-and-fast rule with me, but it is a guideline I find helpful, and evidently others do as well.

When my wife and I went to hear the San Francisco Symphony under the direction of Michael Tilson Thomas, there were pieces by Achille-Claude Debussy and John Adams, as well as Nicolai Rimsky-Korsakov's masterpiece *Scheherezade*. The arrangement was a no-brainer, as the saying goes. If Rimsky-Korsakov's piece had come first, the other selections would have been anticlimactic.

That's why I like to think about the most powerful piece of my sermon coming near the end, if not the very end. For example, when preaching from Mark's story of James and John asking Jesus for a favor when he comes into his kingdom (Mark 10:32–45), the episodic sermon would retell that story in some detail at various points in the sermon—their requesting the places on Jesus' right and left hand, the other disciples' resentment, Jesus' call for his followers to be servants as opposed to rulers, and so forth. The sermon would also include contemporary vignettes, like the play *The Customer Is Always Wrong,* which features tales by waiters about all the rude customers they've served over the years, especially Christians eating out on Sundays after church! There would be slides of exposition, slides of narration, slides of illustrations, slides of application. The first slide, however, would need to be compelling, and the last one even more so. For instance, the final slide might be a textual insight: "Remember how James and John wanted to sit on Jesus' left and right when he came into his glory? Remember? Well, read on in Mark's Gospel. Seems those places were reserved for two thieves." End of sermon. Sermon mapping helps us to decide how the sermon will close.

As for how to select the sermon's origination or beginning, we might choose the second most powerful slide, since the introduction of a sermon is a crucial moment in keeping listeners' attention. But there are other options. Fred Craddock claims that sometimes he starts his sermons in the "shallow end," before inviting listeners into "deeper waters." Deciding how to open the sermon will mean accounting, when possible, for how listeners might best approach the topic of this Sunday's sermon.

Every week preachers face rhetorical decisions of arrangement, and every week the options are staggering. But preaching is not like algebra. The answers are not in the back of the book.

Personal Reflection

How do you feel about the idea of destination and origination? Do you normally save rhetorically powerful material for the conclusion? What about the kind of material you use for the introduction? How do those ideas compare to your normal arrangement of materials? How would you describe your own philosophy of arrangement?

Scriptural Meditation

"Where can I go from your spirit?" (Psalm 139:7)

Playing with the Pieces

Assuming we have some idea as to how the sermon will close and how it will begin, we still have a lot of slides that will comprise the bulk of the sermon. I have found playing with different possibilities to be quite helpful at this point. I remember one pastor, a gifted preacher, asking me with help on a sermon she had recently preached that hadn't "worked." She wanted some feedback on why. I read the manuscript and made only one suggestion—that she simply switch one of the slides near the middle with a slide nearer the end. She agreed that would have made all the difference in the world.

In his book *The Poetry Home Repair Manual*, Ted Kooser suggests that sometimes a poem can be improved by turning it upside down, moving the opening lines to near the end. "You may like your poem a little better when it's standing on its head like that. . . . You can often come up with a better poem by just shifting parts of it around."[29] That is sequencing.

Essayist Thomas Lynch says it's all the same—whether we're arranging flowers on a casket, words on the page of the eulogy, or casseroles on the table in fellowship hall. Arrangement is "an effort at meaning and metaphor, an exercise in symbol and ritualized speech, the heightened acoustics of language raised against what is reckoned unspeakable."[30] This is why newspaper editors debate what will make headlines and what will be buried, what will lead and what will be last. Sequencing matters. Advertising agencies know it, too. Just outside London's Victoria Station I recently saw a wonderfully creative example of playing with sequence. An ad for a trust company, as I recall, it was a very simple billboard, yellow background with black letters on it. The sequence was the message:

"Customers first I like a company that puts its."

Sequencing matters! Therefore, we play with some possible arrangements. We move slides around. We play with the puzzle pieces. We shuffle the deck. However you wish to think of arrangement, all of it's done in an attempt to play with the possibilities.

Will Shorts, the editor of the crossword puzzle for the *New York Times* who has an earned doctorate in puzzles, suggests that playing with arrangement can be the key to solving word games, especially word jumbles like this one for instance:

TERSPEDNI

Shorts suggests that instead of constantly rearranging the letters in a linear fashion, that we arrange them into a pyramid:

T
E R
S P E
D N I

I don't know if that helped you or not, but the answer is "president." I don't know if that suggestion would work homiletically or not either, but creative play is crucial at this stage of sermon preparation.

Creating a sequence is my favorite part of preaching. The playful stage of creating a sequence energizes me. To be honest, however, there are weeks when it's just not happening, at least not very fast. It's helpful at that point to recall a word one artist has coined, "heartbreakthrough," which captures the tension between the waiting, despair, and disappointment, on the one hand, and eventual epiphany and insight that eventually comes, on the other.[31] Still, it is the *heartbreak* part that is so defeating. There are weeks when I look at the two columns and am completely lost. I am not alone, I know. But what then?

In those moments of frustration, I have found that Handel's *Messiah* often helps. You've probably heard of those studies about classical music stimulating thinking, "the Mozart effect." The results are debatable, but for me Handel makes a difference. So does a quick game of solitaire on my computer. The spatial arrangement and sequencing required in solitaire often stimulate my thinking in new ways. Not surprisingly, playing golf helps as well. When we are stuck in matters of creativity, pushing harder is rarely the key. Practices that relax and renew us can be, however, because of their different rhythms. The simple prayer, "Lord, help. I'm stuck," uttered among your prize roses or over a batch of chocolate chip cookie dough, might make the difference for you.

One of the most helpful insights in this regard comes from Robert Dykstra's fascinating book *Discovering a Sermon*. Dykstra claims that *boring* people with our sermons is one of the cardinal sins of preaching but that knowing how to be *bored* is essential for preachers.[32] The first part is obvious enough, but his insight into being bored is truly inspired. Dykstra claims that as preachers we must know how to sit still and play with sermon possibilities, even when nothing seems to be happening. He's right, of course; progress in sermon preparation cannot be measured on the Nasdaq. Some workers in cubicles may have supervisors constantly looking over their shoulders, waiting for measurable results, but the preparation of sermons is different. As Carl Honoré notes in his book *In Praise of Slowness*, "True, the brain can work wonders in high gear. But it will do so much more if given the chance to slow down from time to time."[33]

Oftentimes in the stage of creating a sequence I spend thirty minutes or more reading and rereading my notes without much to show for it. It would be tempting to move on to another task — answering e-mails, returning calls, the list is long. God knows there are other things calling my name, "to dos" needing to get done. Still, I have found that sitting still for thirty minutes at a time, even when nothing much is happening, is crucial. As of today, they don't make a modem slow enough to process spiritual contemplation. Besides, it's hard to know what exactly is happening while we are still. I think about the words of Jesus, "The wind [Spirit] blows where it chooses" (John 3:8). And I think about the words of poet Ted Kooser, who says, "You can learn to love tinkering with drafts of poems [sermons?] till a warm hand from somewhere above you reaches down, unscrews the top of your head, and drops in a solution that blows your ears off."[34]

So let us pray, and let us play. Let us listen, and let us laugh. Let us doodle, too, since creativity is "a process of surrender, not control."[35] And let us wait. Let us wait on the wind to blow.

Personal Reflection

Does the idea of playing with the sermon's pieces trigger creative ideas in you? Look at a recent sermon or this week's sermon as it begins to take shape. How might you rearrange the pieces? What difference would it make in the sermon's feel? What is your reaction to the idea of sitting still with a sermon?

Scriptural Meditation

"Awake, my soul!" (Psalm 108:1)

Renewal
The Sacrament of Music

"What is best about music is not to be found in the notes."
—Gustav Mahler

Afficionados of National Public Radio will remember Noah Adams, former host of *All Things Considered*. What you may not recall is Adams's love for music. Most musical interviews on the program fell to his charge. In fact, Adams took leave from his radio journalism duties to write *Piano Lessons*, a journal of his life-long desire to learn the piano, which he finally undertook at the age of fifty-one. He quotes the celebrated piano teacher David Sudnow, who claims, "Piano playing is the most failed-at social skill in the United States. There are eleven million unused pianos."[36] When I read those words, it occurs to me that those unused pianos have something to say, not just about the failed attempts of so many people to learn piano, but the deep-seated desire in so many of us. We are born to make music, in some fashion or another.

I wonder about all the unused instruments in our closets. I used to play banjo a little, as well as bass guitar. I know preachers who used to play trumpet, flute, saxophone. The list goes on and on. When asked, most people who used to play an instrument, but no longer do, say it's because they've lost their touch. If the idea is not so much a polished performance, the kind our seventh-grade band teacher was aiming for, but the sheer joy of making music, why not dust the cobwebs off and have some fun?

Of course, music making can also take the form of listening to others, on CD or what have you. There have always been people whose greatest accomplishments were aided by listening to music. Most people don't realize, for instance, that Karl Barth was an avid fan of Mozart. Barth claimed, "The theologian who labors without joy is not a theologian at all. Sulky faces, morose thoughts and boring ways of speaking are intolerable in this field." Each morning, before Barth put pen to paper working on his *Church Dogmatics*, he listened to Mozart. He even wrote a book about the musician on the two hundredth anniversary of his birth.

I remember telling the story of Noah Adams's piano adventures in a sermon one Sunday. The story was a metaphor of the joy we long to know in Christ, the unused portions of our lives, or some such emphasis. A few months later I was called to the sanctuary before the service was about to begin. In that particular church the musicians scheduled minirecitals every so often so the children of the church could demonstrate what they were learning. I looked up and saw, among the kids, a middle-aged man I knew, the father of one of the girls. I couldn't figure out why he was up there until after he played Beethoven's "Joyful, Joyful, We Adore Thee." He explained my sermon had inspired him to take up piano. I don't know if I've ever heard more beautiful music.

Whether we are making it, listening to it, or dancing to it, music is, in the words of Martin Luther, "a grand and glorious gift of God." Anybody feel like making music?

Preacher Dates

— Invite friends over and listen to each other's favorite music
— Attend the opera or symphony
— Dust off an old instrument or take up a new one and make some music
— Sing along with some of your favorite recording artists
— Rent *Amadeus* and watch it with the sound turned way up
— Visit a music store and find a recording you've always wanted to own

> *"Music is the mediator between the spiritual and the sensual life."*
> —Ludwig van Beethoven

SIX

STAGE FOUR: EMBODYING THE SERMON

"God loves you . . . but don't let it go to your heads."

The Sermon Becomes Flesh

Shortly after the actor Christopher Reeve's death, National Public Radio aired a previously recorded interview. Best known for his role as Superman, he had been paralyzed for nearly ten years after a horseback riding accident. Ironies were noted, of course, like how a man once able to leap tall buildings was now unable to walk. Not surprisingly, the interview was emotionally packed. Reeve admitted to occasional bouts of jealousy regarding other people's health, even the simple act of standing to stretch. He wondered aloud if folks realize how fortunate they are to stand at all, the sacredness of bodily movement. He recalled the sheer joy when, after years of treatment, he suddenly could move his left index finger. Listening to that interview, I remember feeling goose bumps as he spoke, a bodily sensation in themselves.

Fully appreciated, preaching is one of those rich bodily movements in which we are blessed to participate. I know some preachers who, like the comedians Johnny Carson and Robin Williams, can do wonders during a sermon just with their eyebrows. Bodily movement. I know other preachers who, although healthy, seem paralyzed in the pulpit on Sundays. Preaching is a bodily act, the moment when we embody the sermon.

Both terms are worth noting: *embodying* and *sermon*. I'm using the former in place of the more customary term, sermon *delivery*. As Richard Ward declares, "Delivery is what Pizza Hut does; and sermons aren't pizzas!" Over the past few years Ward and others have proposed the term *performing* instead.[1] I know, *performance* seems too shallow a term, too showy. But not necessarily. The word itself literally means "to bring to completion" or "to bring the form through." Still, most preachers—and a lot of congregations— wince when they hear something about performing the sermon.

That's too bad, because while delivery and performance have their shadow sides, they are also wonderfully evocative terms in the right context. For instance, while we have our pizzas delivered, doctors also deliver babies. That context can hardly be construed as impersonal and trivial, and birthing is a wonderful metaphor for preaching, as some notable women preachers have observed.[2] And while actors perform their lines, doctors also perform surgeries, a term that among other things denotes precision, even an art form. In some circles ministers are said not just to officiate at a wedding, but to perform a wedding.

Still, I have come to prefer the term *embodying* because ultimately preaching is delivered or performed as a bodily act. The preacher is bodily present before the gathered body of Christ. We speak words that are carried on our breath across the room into the ears of listeners. Imagine that: our words enter the bodies of the congregation. "We speak in tongues./My mouth to your ear," writes Julia Cameron in her poem "Body Language."[3] No wonder sometimes a person leaving church will say how our sermon *touched* them. That's what preaching does.

Consider the embodied sermon in light of the Genesis creation accounts. In the first story (Genesis 1) God speaks and marvelous things happen. God says, "Light," and there is light, bright and illuminating. God says, "Golden retriever," and it wags its tail. God speaks and things happen in the first creation story. In the second creation story (Genesis 2) God moves from speaking to touching. Clay is thrown on the potter's wheel, so to speak, and all the angels gather round to see what God is making. Of course, what God's hands are making, dirty and caked as they are, is human beings. But humans are not fully brought into being until the divine breath enters them. God breathes life into us.

The best theology I know for the sermon as preached is when these two stories come together—there is speaking and there is the divine breath. And things happen. Creation happens anew! When a human being (insert your name here) stands before the gathered community to preach (insert your body here) that is when a *sermon* happens, that second all-important term. All week long we are working on what we hope will be a sermon, but it is not really a sermon until embodied in the context of the body of Christ gathered in worship.

Personal Reflection

What bodily movements do you enjoy most? How might you incorporate that joy bodily into your preaching? What term do you prefer for the giving of a sermon? Delivering? Performing? Embodying? What do the two Genesis stories say to you about preaching and the body? Are there other scriptural stories and images that come to mind?

Scriptural Meditation

> *"How beautiful are the feet of those who bring good news!"*
> *(Romans 10:15)*

—————————————————————————————
—————————————————————————————
—————————————————————————————
—————————————————————————————
—————————————————————————————
—————————————————————————————
—————————————————————————————
—————————————————————————————
—————————————————————————————
—————————————————————————————

The Sacred but Scary Truth

Every year at Advent we are reminded that Jesus did not become flesh in theory but actually dwelt among us—"pitched his tent," as some have translated that first chapter of John's Gospel (1:14). That is the sacred truth. But the notion that we too are somehow to incarnate, or flesh out, the gospel when we preach is not only sacred but more than a bit scary. It can be downright frightening!

Imagine a bunch of preachers gathered in a workshop setting. One at a time, we are invited to stand before the group. Just stand there, that's all. As your turn approaches, you can sense the tension mounting—a bodily sensation. You stand, and after what seems an eternity—say, thirty seconds or so—you sit down. The next person stands. Around the room it goes. What exactly happens when we stand before others, which is of course what we do every time we preach?

Most of us are never sure where to look, what to do, especially what to do with these appendages we call arms and hands. Even if we wear a robe on Sunday, we are never hidden. Even if some well-meaning deacon or elder offers a prayer that the preacher might be hidden behind the cross and Jesus made known, we are still there, right in front of God and everybody gathered. I do this exercise with my students—having them stand in front of us, one at a time—and it is always awkward.

Truth is, we are very sensitive about our bodies; some features we like and others we wish we could change. The tendency in Western cultures in particular is to think of the body solely in sexual terms. All those magazines at the grocery store checkout probably contribute to such thinking. Granted, we are sexual beings, but more fundamentally we are human beings. Created by God, we are more than bodies, but we are bodies. And our bodies function in many ways. Our bodies eat and on occasion pass gas—we hope not during the sermon—though most of us recall times in which we had to fight off a belch or two as breakfast came back to haunt us. Our bodies take us places. Our bodies get sick. Our bodies sleep—maybe not enough—though we hope our congregants' bodies don't while we're preaching.

I recall hearing Barbara Brown Taylor lecture to a large crowd of ministers and talk about her body. She began, "No doubt, you have noticed I'm rather tall. You've noticed that my hair which was once prematurely grey is still that color. You've noticed my nose, my eyes . . ." In a playful but serious spirit, she asked us as preachers to revel in our God-given bodies, through which we preach the gospel.

Anne Lamott tells about going to hear a most unusual preacher give a talk at a benefit for refugees in Kosovo. She met David Roche on the phone, and he described himself as having a facial deformity, but she wasn't really prepared for the shock of it all. David was born with a benign tumor on the left side of his face, and surgeries and radiation resulted in his face being covered with what Lamott describes as "plum-colored burns." His deformities were part of what he wanted to talk about. He suggested that the audience ask him in unison, "David, what happened to your face?" And after they asked, he told his story "through a crazy mouth, a jumble of teeth, only one lip, and a too-large tongue."

Then David Roche got down to business, so to speak. Here is Lamott's summary of his talk:

"We with facial deformities are children of the dark," he said. "Our shadow is on the outside. And we can see in the dark: we can see you, we see you turn away, but one day we finally understand that you turn away not from our faces but from your own fears. From those things inside you that you think mark you as someone unlovable to your family, and society, and even to God."

Lamott adds, "David spoke of the hidden scary scarred parts inside us all, the soul disfigurement, the fear deep within us that we're unacceptable; and while he spoke, his hands moved fluidly in expressions that his face can't make. His hands are beautiful, fair, light as air, light as a ballet dancer's."[4]

Whether we are Hollywood material or not, God invites us to revel in our bodies. Perhaps some of us are embarrassed by certain features—thinning hair or a growing waistline. Or maybe we are encouraged by a thinning waistline, thanks to a low-carb diet. Be that as it may, these bodies are us. We are more than bodies, but we are bodies.

Personal Reflection

What strikes you the most about your body as a vehicle for the gospel? What do you like about your body? Dislike? In what ways does your self-image help you preach? In what ways does it hinder your preaching?

Scriptural Meditation

"Let everything that breathes praise the LORD!" (Psalm 150:6)

Hide Me behind Something

Ask any group of preachers about the act of preaching, and at least one of them will eventually say something about the pulpit. Pulpits are too tall these days. Too short. Too small. Way too large! I once heard Fred Craddock preach from behind a Plexiglas pulpit. In his opening remarks he said, "Well, I guess preachers who stand behind glass pulpits probably shouldn't throw stones." There are some see-through pulpits here and there but more of the solid wood variety. So a good number of preachers, in an attempt at being more present, have started preaching without pulpits when possible. They move freely about on the chancel platform. Some come down to the floor, others even out into the congregation. A chapel speaker at our seminary went so far into the congregation that folks on the first few rows had to turn around to see the preacher. The preacher was preaching behind their backs.

Some preachers do indeed walk about, but not in every church, of course. Some congregations simply won't have it; the preacher's place is in the pulpit, so they claim. Some PA systems require that the minister stay put in the pulpit. Some preachers are reluctant to come out from behind that symbol of authority for theological reasons or from behind that symbol of refuge for reasons more psychological. For some, the pulpit is like the oak tree we called base in a kid's game of hide-and-seek, a place of security.

The truth is, we preachers are just as likely to be present behind a massive pulpit as we are to be hiding when out in the open. It's not the furniture or the lack thereof that makes the difference. What parishioners seek in their preachers—regardless of where they stand to preach—is authenticity. And rightly or wrongly, parishioners are quite willing to make that judgment call. I've learned most ministers are willing, too. I sometimes show a video-tape to preachers, excerpts from twenty sermons by twenty different preachers—various nationalities, men and women, robed and not, different denominational traditions.[5] Each clip is only ten to twenty seconds in length; yet ministers viewing the tape are more than willing to label which preachers seem authentically present and which ones do not. More amazingly, as a group we are almost always unanimous in our verdicts.[6] What does that tell you?

Using those same video clips we also think about the color of the preacher, not literally but metaphorically. Ron Hoff's quirky book about making "great presentations" in business and elsewhere invites us to consider how speeches—sermons—come in three main colors: blue, red, and gray.[7] I've applied his descriptions to preaching. Blue preachers are orderly and disciplined. They're analytical, logical, rational, and restrained. Blue preachers capture the attention of the congregation by their precision. Red preachers are more charged in their manner. They are emotional, driven, charismatic, even impulsive at times. Red preachers are more passionate than precise.

Gray preachers are none of these things. They're not so much somewhere between blue and red, but somewhere underneath. Gray preachers are a dime a dozen, because being gray is a safe place from which to preach, and because gray is what many churches have come to expect. In truth, it is possible to hide while preaching, to hide behind a mask of dull and drab gray.

Personal Reflection

Think about your pulpit for a moment. How would you describe it? What features in particular do you like about it? Dislike? How might subtle changes be made to it? Do you normally stay behind it or move around on the chancel? When was the last time you watched yourself preaching on videotape? What did you notice about your movement? What color is your style of preaching? Do you want to be a different color?

Scriptural Meditation

> *"Rejoice and exult with all your heart, O daughter Jerusalem!"*
> *(Zephaniah 3:14)*

Renewal
The Sacrament of Movement

*"All sanity depends on this: that it should be a delight to feel
heat strike the skin, a delight to stand upright,
knowing the bones are moving easily under the flesh."*
–Doris Lessing[8]

When we were kids, some of us not only played with Gumby, that
flexible green man with his orange horse Pokey, we could bend
our bodies like the two of them as well. Remember? As we get
older, we're more like Humpty Dumpty. If we fall, something's
likely to break, and all the king's horses and all the king's men may
not be able to put us back together again. There is a need in us, a
bodily need, to move in a whole range of motions.

The options between running the Boston Marathon and running back to the kitchen for another piece of Boston cream pie are
too numerous to count. We don't have to hire a personal trainer
and take up Pilates — although that sounds appealing — but neither
do we have to resign ourselves to one more doughnut at the next
ministerial alliance meeting because we've been working hard
lately. In *The Power of Full Engagement*, their fascinating book on the
management of energy, not time, Jim Loehr and Tony Schwartz
remind us that if we push ourselves mentally, emotionally, and
spiritually, but neglect physical exercise, we will break eventually.[9] Too busy? Brother David Steindl-Rast reminds us that the
Chinese character for "busy" comes from two words, *heart* and
killing.[10]

Although a counterintuitive notion, most of us realize that the
more stressed out and tired we are, the better we feel after a brisk
walk or swim. That's why they called those courses we took in
school, physical *education*. We were supposed to learn something
about the importance of being physical in this world.

On our twenty-fifth wedding anniversary, my wife and I went
to New York City for a few days. We saw *Phantom of the Opera*, had
drinks in the Rainbow Room where Meg Ryan saw her love atop
the Empire State Building in *Sleepless in Seattle*, and nearly walked
ourselves to death all over Manhattan. One night on the Lower

East Side, we were eating seafood on the deck of a restaurant, when we spied hundreds of people just down the shoreline, dancing. It was some sort of dance contest, with a definite Latin flavor to it. They were having such fun, moving to the rhythms of the music. Do you like to dance?

Preacher Dates

— Take a martial arts course just for fun; you don't have to earn a black belt
— Try yoga or other stretching exercises, beginning with the simplest of moves
— Swim laps at the local indoor pool, or an outdoor one in summer
— Take up ballroom dancing, or disco if you prefer
— Play Twister: "Right foot, red. Left hand, blue."
— Go for a bike ride through your neighborhood or on a trail
— Do some "jumping jacks" and feel your blood flow

"To live is to dance, to dance is to live."
—Snoopy[11]

"The only way we experience creation — life, whether at its most beautiful or its harshest — is through our own bodies and the bodies of other people."
—Mary Cartledgehayes[12]

The Center of Attention

Lots of preachers I know read and savored every page of Marilynne Robinson's Pulitzer Prize–winning novel *Gilead*. I can only assume they also noted the many references to one of the pressing questions for the narrator, a preacher himself. The Reverend John Ames repeatedly wonders about all those sermons he preached over the years. "There are boxes of them in the attic, a few recent years of them in stacks in the closet," he writes. "I've never gone back to them to see if they were worth anything, if I actually said anything. Pretty nearly my whole life's work is in those boxes, which is an amazing thing to reflect on." And later, "It's humiliating to have written as much as Augustine, and then to have to find a way to dispose of it." And near the end of the novel there is one last poignant passage about all those sermons:

> I'll just ask your mother to have those old sermons of mine burned. The deacons could arrange it. There are enough to make a good fire. I'm thinking here of hot dogs and marshmallows, something to celebrate the first snow. Of course she can set by any of them she might want to keep, but I don't want her to waste much effort on them. They mattered or they didn't and that's the end of it.[13]

Most of us recognize this condition: PDS, Preacher Distress Syndrome. In this case, a preoccupation with all those sermons, wondering if any of them mattered. We know that the preaching ministry is not about us, yet we are so involved in it. So sometimes we hide, behind pulpits, or robes, or masks of piety, or stained-glass voices. Anywhere we can. Equally tragic, if not more so, are the preachers who are all too present, the kind listeners wish would hide somewhere.

But if preaching truly is a bodily act, there is no choice but to be present. The question is, How present? Next time you hear someone else preach, try to identify the center of attention. By that, I mean try to note where the primary focus is in the room during the sermon. Who or what is the center? Is it the manuscript from which the preacher is reading? The gathered people of God? Is it the biblical text on which the sermon is based? The preacher?[14] The center can change many times in the midst of a given sermon, but where is it?

As easy as it is for most of us to identify the preacher as too central when listening to someone else preach, it is much more difficult to identify that center when we are the preacher. We have other things to occupy our attention in that moment. This might be one of those times when asking a colleague to watch a videotape would be helpful. Or maybe a control group within the congregation, although we should be careful not to "ruin" the worship experience for them. Same for a friend or family member, too. Still, an honest critique by others might be just the thing we need. None of us want to be the center of attention, not really.

Personal Reflection

What do you hope is the center of attention when you preach? How would you describe your aspirations in that regard? Think about one of your favorite preachers. How is she or he present in the sermon? What do you think about asking others to assess your presence?

Scriptural Meditation

"You desire truth in the inward being." (Psalm 51:6)

Best Supporting Actress

Most years at the Academy Awards presenters make a point of clarifying that the Oscar for, say, Best Supporting Actress should read, "the best performance by an actress in a supporting role." The distinction is more than semantics. These supporting roles, the characters they play on the screen, are done in support of the main characters. It's what literary buffs will recall is the difference between round and flat characters. Moviegoers aren't supposed to notice the supporting cast as much as the leading characters. For that matter, moviegoers aren't supposed to notice that anybody on the screen is acting. As long as audiences keep marveling at Jamie Foxx's portrayal of Ray Charles, the actor has failed. Getting audiences to think they're watching the real thing: that's the goal.

Similar dynamics are at work in our preaching, and not just the possibility congregants might perceive us as the center of attention. No, there are other aspects of embodying the sermon in which the goal is supporting something bigger. Namely, our gestures, mannerisms, eye contact, use of silence, and a whole host of bodily movements can help support our preaching—or not. When I went to seminary, the word of choice was *delivery*, and the professor kept reminding us, "Delivery supports content." Although I no longer prefer the term *delivery*, the concept holds true. So when we preachers wonder about a whole host of practical questions—like "Is it ever appropriate to whisper when preaching?" "What are some guidelines for the use of gestures?" "What should I do with my hands?" "Where should I look during my sermon?"—the answer is almost always the same: embodiment supports content.

I remember a seminary student's sermon in class in which we encouraged him to think about quickening his rate of speaking at times. Not always, but sometimes—when the sermon warranted it. He was from the South, with a slow drawl, and was pretty laid back on top of that. You've heard of type A and type B personalities? He was a type Z. In the midst of his sermon he'd told about a Thanksgiving dinner at his grandmother's during which the house caught on fire. When he described the chaos and confusion of family members and pets scurrying to get out, the pace was so slow that most of us were amazed he had made it out himself. His rate of speech did not sound on fire.

This principle of our embodiment supporting the content is a wonderful clue for us preachers. Just as stage directions in the script provide clues for actors, the content of our sermons—the words we hope to say—provides clues for our embodiment. And the biblical text is the key. If the textual narrative is intimate—the risen Lord uttering Mary's name in the garden—so should our presentation be. That means looking at our parishioners, speaking softly, slowly. If our Lord has been raised, and the women have been told to proclaim that good news to the others, that's a different story, one that calls for a different kind of storytelling, urgent and animated.

Personal Reflection

What specific issues of embodying the sermon do you struggle with? Eye contact? Gestures? Facial expressions? What to do with your hands? How might the idea of "embodiment supporting content" make a difference? Look at the text for this week. What embodiment clues are embedded there? What clues are embedded in your sermon? How might these clues impact your preaching this Sunday?

Scriptural Meditation

"My soul thirsts for God, for the living God." (Psalm 42:2)

To Write or Not to Write?

If sermons are acoustical events that happen at a moment in time when Christ's body is gathered for worship, can sermons really be written down? The simple answer is no; not if we understand a sermon to be an embodied act. But we may wish to write out what we hope, with the Spirit's breath, will become a sermon in our speaking, come Sunday. As Frederick Buechner observes, writing a sermon is an attempt "to put the Gospel into word not the way you would compose an essay but the way you would write a poem or a love letter — putting your heart into it, your own excitement, most of all your own life."[15]

Before I attended seminary I never dreamed of writing a manuscript. I prepared as thoroughly as I knew how, scribbling out pages and pages of thoughts, but as Sunday approached, it all got translated into a page or two of detailed notes, never anything more. When, on the first day of preaching class in seminary, the professor informed us that all our assignments would be manuscripts, written out word for word, I couldn't imagine how that was possible. As I pondered, I saw his point. How could my little notes that read "story about my dog" or "Luke's emphasis on inclusion" make any sense to him or his graduate assistant? Still, I wasn't sure. Of course, I eventually learned how to write out my sermons, or else I would still be enrolled, but it was not easy. I figured once I graduated I could go back to my old ways, like leading a horse to water, but drinking being another matter.

Amazingly, however, shortly after taking that course, I could no longer fathom preparing a sermon without writing a manuscript. I have been writing manuscripts ever since, sometimes even for a short devotional prepared for a Wednesday night gathering or the like. And like my mentor, I require students to write out their sermons word for word, even though it may not be what they will do in the "real world" once they've graduated. So what are the benefits of a manuscript?

For starters, the practice of writing helps to sharpen our thoughts. Ask anyone to tell a story impromptu — even a familiar one like how they met their spouse or partner — and the chances are the telling will include more than a few sentences that begin, "Oh, I forgot to mention . . ." "I forgot to mention the part about our friend who reluctantly introduced us to each other . . ." "I forgot to mention how we didn't hit it off right away . . ."

Moreover, even if we remember all the details and in the right order, the chances are that our word choices could be better. True, a written sermon is only twenty-six letters strategically arranged, but the possibilities are limitless, both for good and ill. Consider Thomas Merton's observation on what it means to write well for God: "A bad book about the love of God remains a bad book, even though it may be about the love of God. There are many who think that because they have written about God, they have written good books."[16] Same goes for sermons. Every computer includes a Delete key, and for very good reasons. Not only that, but sitting at a computer and searching for the best word for the right moment can enhance our ability to find the right word when in our preaching we ad lib something.

I recently visited with a seminary student serving as a part-time associate minister. She was just beginning her preaching ministry, trying to find her own way. She confessed to a degree of shame and embarrassment for preaching from manuscripts, that maybe preaching wasn't for her. That is, until she heard Barbara Brown Taylor preach, with a manuscript. She shared that as a result of that encounter, shame had given way to affirmation.

Of course, not all preachers write out their sermons. Not even the best preachers. Fred Craddock writes down phrases here and there that he intends to use in the midst of a story or certain section of exposition, but not the whole sermon. He says some editors have asked him from time to time for a copy of a sermon they heard him preach so they might publish it. They are usually incredulous when he informs them no such copy exists. He tells them, "You can transcribe it if you like, but I don't have it written out." Craddock is not alone. Part of our journey as preachers is discovering whether writing out the whole sermon, parts of the sermon, or none of the sermon works best for us.

Personal Reflection

What is your normal practice regarding writing out the sermon? Word for word? Pieces of the sermon, perhaps the introduction or some other crucial segment? None of it? Has your approach changed over the years? What caused such a change? Have you considered experimenting with another way?

"The unfolding of your words gives light." (*Psalm 119:130*)

Walking on Water

If you've never tried preaching without notes, even the idea can be horrifying. The stuff nightmares are made of, only instead of that recurring dream about preaching with no clothes on, it's with no notes on — no notes on the pulpit or scribbled on a note card. I think about that story in which Jesus comes to the disciples walking on water (Matthew 14:22–33). Allow me a brief playful retelling:

> Recognizing Jesus, Peter wants to do the same — to preach without notes. He gets out of the boat and, who knows, maybe walking on water is more exciting than anything we can imagine — except for preaching without notes. Maybe he steps over the waves, or maybe they crash about him as he walks, but he strolls on top of a stormy sea — never once losing his train of thought. Then he sees the wind — realizes he's preaching without notes — and begins to sink, to stammer about in the pulpit.

While the idea of preaching without notes can be horrifying, it holds out possibilities of exhilaration, too — like learning to ride a bike for the first time. Pure adrenalin. I think about the story homiletician Charles Campbell tells, of the female seminarian who enrolled in a class he and a New Testament colleague were teaching. Students were required to preach in a public place. The idea was to perform "the Scriptures in the urban context." She believed in the cause and in her message, but eventually realized that preaching in such a context would mean, among other things, preaching without notes. In a letter to her boyfriend, she described just how exhilarating the whole enterprise became:

> I wanted to say something else about the sermon. What you might be able to relate to is the challenge of doing something that scares you to death—like skiing on a steep slope, or hang-gliding, or bungee-jumping, or anything that involves a risk. When you are able to do it, you feel exhilarated because a challenge has been met; the obstacle of fear has been overcome. Have you ever experienced that?[17]

I remember with great delight when a former student of mine preached her first sermon without notes. Her name was Day, and the brightness of her name described her affect. When informed of the assignment to preach without notes, she threw her hands up and scoffed in a good-natured sort of way. She asked if I realized how old she was, or how she sometimes can't remember where she parked when she runs into the grocery store, or even what she is in there to buy. I laughed with her, and later celebrated with her as well. The whole class did. Moments after embodying her sermon without notes, she threw herself onto the first pew in the chapel and collapsed in joy. Day had won the day! When I wrote her, asking permission to tell her story, Day said she didn't remember it so much as a "great accomplishment, but as an exercise in trust . . . a free-floating and vulnerable experience!" That testimony has been repeated over and over by ministers I know, those willing to take the leap.

Personal Reflection

So how scared are you to try preaching without notes? How curious are you about the possibilities? Can you imagine walking on water, really walking on water? What about preaching without notes? Have you ever tried it? Maybe even by accident? What happened?

Scriptural Meditation

"Take heart, it is I; do not be afraid." (Matthew 14:27)

How to Walk on Water

You may be wondering why anyone who advocates writing manuscripts could possibly advocate preaching without notes. Contrary to popular opinion, the two ideas are not at odds. Let me explain.

In one of the preaching classes I teach, I inform the group that in addition to preaching in some local churches during the semester, each of them will preach three times before their peers. I tell them that for the first assignment in class the only "notes" they can use is a manuscript. It can be highlighted or not. They can read it or ignore it, but that's it. The second assignment, I tell them, is to be preached without notes. Once they've recovered from their fainting spell and had a glass of water, I repeat, "Without notes.

Just you and your Bible. No sticky notes, either. The third sermon," I continue, "will need to be somewhere between those two extremes." I leave that decision up to each of them.

Well, them and the videotape. Only occasionally do those who are accustomed to preaching from a manuscript find the process very effective when they see themselves on tape. "I guess I do tend to look down a lot," they concede. "I thought I sounded more natural than that." Or "My body is hardly even involved." These are some of the more common responses—these and wanting to hide.

As the time comes for them to preach without notes, they no longer want to hide. Instead, some want to jump off a bridge. I take them into our chapel and there at the pulpit assure them no one has ever died on this spot. I assure them we will learn some techniques. For starters, we read Joseph Webb's helpful book, *Preaching without Notes*. Webb contends that such an approach requires a different mindset from the very beginning of sermon preparation, not just on the weekend.[18]

If the sermon's sequence doesn't flow well or logically, remembering becomes increasingly difficult. As an example, biblical storyteller Dennis Dewey teaches workshops in which he shows how to remember a list of ten random items:

an apple
an orange
a baby elephant
a three-legged piano stool
a bed of daffodils
a white picket fence
a large cardboard box
a platter of fettuccine Alfredo
a gold Visa card
a red jeep in need of a tune-up

Dewey then asks who can recall all ten items, in order. Close the book a moment and see how you do. It's not easy, is it? I heard him recite this list twice, and I have yet to forget it even though it's been years ago now. The reason I remember it is his second telling of the list, the one in which he spins a narrative around the items.

Dewey asks participants to picture an apple, red and shiny with a tiny leaf on top. The apple is balanced on top of an orange. He then asks us to imagine both pieces of fruit balanced on the trunk of a baby elephant. The elephant itself is delicately balanced atop the piano stool, a three-legged stool. Surrounding the stool is a bed of daffodils, and surrounding the flowers is a white picket fence. The wind has blown a large cardboard box against the fence. Sitting atop the box is a large platter of fettuccine Alfredo, and coming out of the pasta is a gold Visa card. Next to all of this is a sputtering red jeep, desperately in need of a tune-up. Go ahead, close the book now and give it another try. You might even read the above narrative aloud. It makes a difference because now we have a metanarrative to hold the items together. That, claims Webb, is how our sermons must be arranged if we are to preach without notes and recall our material. The sequence must flow logically or, better yet, narratively.[19]

Both of our daughters take dance—tap and jazz—and they tell me it's nearly impossible to memorize a particular dance step in the *middle* of a routine. They have to go through the sequences that lead up to that step. Any minister who has ever sat on the chancel platform knows the panic that can set in just before preaching. *Will I remember that story in the middle? What comes after that?* We do well to trust the power of sequencing and that God will be with us. It also helps, as one of my students noted, that the congregation is not like those figure-skating judges at the Olympics, the ones who have before them an outline of the routine to be skated. Parishioners do not have to know if we forget a certain section.

Webb also claims that the decision to preach a sermon without notes should be made early in the week, not late, because of the time we will need to rehearse the sermon. Rehearsing is rather difficult if on Saturday we're still writing it. I know some ministers whose rehearsal occurs at home, silently looking over the sermon. I have a good friend who goes to the church every Saturday evening and preaches it aloud in the sanctuary. Rehearsing is essential, especially when we preach without notes.

As for some techniques—Robert Frost's "technical tricks"—on preaching without notes, the key for me is thought blocks. Thought blocks are the units or pieces of our sermons, the slides of our show, to use a metaphor we considered before. Analyze most sermons, and you will find on average ten to twelve thought blocks. Any given block might be contained in a single paragraph or span a couple of paragraphs. A story from the week's news would constitute a thought block, as would your exegetical observations on verse 13. Those are thought blocks.

Most of us forget what we want to say, not in the middle of our thought blocks, but in between them, during the transitions. For instance, we're retelling that news story that's on everyone's mind: "You saw the video of the subway crash, the twisted metal. I read in one account that a lady . . . uh, a lady . . ." Blank. No, that's not what happens. We remember what happened, what the lady said, and so forth. The real tension develops as we reach the end of that story and try to recall what comes next. The problem is not with our thought blocks but the transitions between them.

For that reason, instead of imagining how you're going to memorize Sunday's sermon, think in terms of memorizing the flow of your thought blocks. "I start with that quote, then a piece of textual background, the story about my aunt, Mark's use of an inclusio . . ." If we can name the basic flow of our thought blocks, we are on the way to preaching without notes. Personally, I find it helpful to go for a walk as I practice the sermon's flow and progression of thought blocks. Let's face it, if we're going to preach the sermon without notes on Sunday, we probably need to see if we can do it before then. My two dogs and I go for a walk around the lake near our house. I preach it in my head, rarely aloud. I have tried speaking it aloud, but the dogs always look too confused. On those occasions when I can't recall what's next, I press on with what I can recall and, when I get back home, look up what I forgot. Sometimes the fault lies with my memory, other times with the flow of the sermon itself, which needs minor adjustments. Walking is crucial at this stage, not just because there are no notes with me to look at, but because it is bodily, and so will be the preaching moment on Sunday.

Probably the hardest aspect of preaching without notes is how it adds one more dimension to the week's preparation. In other words, while Craddock maintains that preachers need to have two eurekas—exegetical and homiletical—if listeners are going to have one, preaching without notes requires a third eureka, the moment when, having practiced the sermon enough, we can exclaim, "I've got it!" There are weeks in my own preaching ministry when I think it would be so much easier just to take the manuscript with me into the pulpit. Preaching without notes, like a lot of things in life, demands great energy. But the rewards are well worth it, like learning to ride a bike—with no hands!

Personal Reflection

Have you ever watched a videotape of your preaching? What did you notice about your use of notes? Look at a sermon you preached recently. How much of it do you recall without notes? How many thought blocks do you detect? Look at your sermon for this Sunday. Try to identify the thought blocks and recall their progression.

Scriptural Meditation

"You shall go out in joy, and be led back in peace." (Isaiah 55:12)

Renewal
The Sacrament of Bread and Wine

"Come quickly! I am tasting stars."
—Don Pérignon[20]

"In water one sees one's own face;
But in wine one beholds the heart of another."
—Old French Proverb[21]

Adapting the Jewish tradition of a Passover meal, Christians eat the Sunday meal called Eucharist, a sacred meal of bread and wine. But in many ways, all our meals are sacred; and bread and wine take on different forms—milk and cookies, coffee and donuts, champagne and strawberries, even beer and pretzels. In his fascinating book *How to Read Literature like a Professor*, Thomas Foster contends that meal scenes in literature always signal a Eucharist of sorts, "Once or twice a semester at least I will stop discussion of the story or play under consideration to intone (and I invariably intone in bold): **Whenever people eat or drink together, it's communion.**"[22]

"To eat is still something more than to maintain bodily functions," observes Alexander Schmemann. "People may not understand what that 'something more' is, but they nonetheless desire to celebrate it. They are still hungry and thirsty for sacramental life."[23] There is a sacredness to food. How vividly I recall all the meals we ate with our good friends Ronnie and Rhonda while in seminary together, and especially the evening our first child was born and the meal later that night. When my wife had gone to sleep for the night, Ronnie and Rhonda took me to our favorite pizza shop to get a bite to eat. It was only some Italian sausage, cheese, and tomato sauce on dough, but it was so much more. All these years later both our families still treasure the many meals we ate together. As the poet Bobi Jones puts it, "Breaking words over food is somehow different from customary chatting."[24]

In her book *Breaking Bread: The Spiritual Significance of Food*, Sara Covin Juengst notes that even if our dining room tables are rectangular, eating together is always a "circular action." We *gather around* the food we eat, even as the food gathers us in.[25]

Preacher Dates

— Enjoy a breakfast cereal you haven't had since you were a kid
— Watch the movie *Babette's Feast* while feasting with some dear friends
— Recall a favorite blessing and say it over a favorite meal
— Buy a copy of Maya Angelou's cookbook; the recipes include stories
— Bake some bread from scratch and enjoy it with a glass of wine or favorite beverage
— Invite some "strangers" to your table for a meal and conversation

> *"Most people eat as if they were fattening themselves for market."*
> —Edgar Watson Howe[26]

> *"Food is the daily sacrament of unnecessary goodness, ordained for a continual remembrance that the world will always be more delicious than it is useful."*
> —Robert Farrar Capon[27]

Presence vs. Precision

"Some weeks I really love what I've written. Not relying on my manuscript would mean botching up some beautiful lines I've written." I can't tell you how many times I've heard ministers say something like this. It's not just fear of forgetting in general that makes us preachers hesitant to preach without notes. Some preachers are writers. Some ministers know how to turn a phrase, to paint a lovely word picture. So naturally the idea of giving up the manuscript is more than threatening; it's depressing. *Why bother with the craft of writing, if I'm simply going to hem and haw in the pulpit?* "And, uh, in the eleventh verse, I mean, when I was reading the other day, I mean . . ."

Such a concern is legitimate. You don't have to be a Pulitzer Prize–winning author to appreciate the words you've crafted. I think of this tension in terms of presence vs. precision. We want to be present, to have good eye contact, to avoid reading our manuscript to the church, but occasionally we feel a fondness for the precision of our syntax, the concrete verbs, a lovely alliterated line, at least parts of the manuscript. Presence vs. precision.

In such a battle, however, it's no contest. Presence always wins out over precision, because preaching is bodily, a time when we are present. I can't tell you how many times churchgoers have complained to me as a teacher of preachers about their minister reading the sermon to them. "I know how to read, thank you very much. Don't they realize we're in the sanctuary with them, not out in radioland?"

Imagine a paragraph in Sunday's sermon of which you are especially fond. Maybe there is one particular image or line that you can't imagine omitting. What I'm contending is that even if you don't get it word for word, your presence and passion will more than make up for it. But then again, why must we choose between presence and precision? Why not be present *and* precise? I'm not implying that we memorize the whole sermon. Who has the time for that? What I am suggesting is that we memorize the sections we are most fond of.

Actually, the word *memorize* may not be quite right. What we really seek is to *internalize* the content of our sermons. There is a huge difference between the two. Think about the poems you memorized in grade school—the ones you never missed a word reciting, but that also never spoke to your soul. I suspect the poems you have memorized as an adult are different. They say something to your deepest recesses. You know them *by heart*.

I recall the painful experience of one of my students when he preached without notes in class. He was about halfway through the message, going along nicely, when he went blank. He couldn't remember what was next. Nothing. He hesitated. We all felt sorry for him. Silent prayers went up. All of this in a moment. After ten seconds or so of silence—a lifetime when you're in the pulpit—he finally said to me, "I can't remember what's next." I assured him that it was OK. "Just take your time. Perhaps you might want to start that section over. Don't worry about it." He tried again.

Nothing. Finally I asked, "What are you trying to say to us? What is God's message you have for us?" He started to respond in general terms, speaking from his heart. I said, "Preach that. Preach what's on your heart."

Personal Reflection

How would you describe your attachment to the words you write for Sundays? When you watch yourself preach on videotape, which is usually dominant, presence or precision? Are there some sections of your sermons (stories, for example) in which you are more present? More precise? How does the notion of "speaking from your heart" sound?

Scriptural Meditation

"Come, bless the LORD." (Psalm 134:1)

The Middle Ground

Reading some homiletics books, you can get the impression that we preachers are either reading our manuscripts to the congregation — and in a dull monotone, no less — or we are dynamic preachers who never use notes—which some choir members always find impressive. There is a middle ground, to be sure, and that middle ground is more expansive than the distance between the biblical east and west.

Some preachers have always written manuscripts and used them in the pulpit to one degree or another. Other preachers have always preached without notes, some never missing a beat, others faking it on occasion. The middle-ground approach acknowledges the strengths of manuscripts on the one hand and freedom from notes on the other hand, while seeking to borrow from both approaches.

In the middle-ground approach, we still probably should think in terms of thought blocks. The difference is that instead of having to memorize the progression of those blocks, we write down some "triggers" that will jump-start our brains. In other words, on Saturday, for instance, the preacher sets the manuscript to the side and places a 3 x 5 card before her. She looks through the manuscript to identify the first thought block and then jots down a couple of words intended to trigger her memory. After she's done that for the ten or so thought blocks, the key is to test those blocks. She looks at the first one and starts preaching in her head. When she gets to the end of that block, she looks at the next one. She keeps doing this as long as the triggers work. If she looks at her trigger on the note card and wonders, "What in the world does that mean?" then she simply returns to the manuscript and determines a better trigger.

Talking to preachers over the years, I've observed great variety when it comes to notes systems. Everything from those sticky notes—upside down in their Bibles so they flip toward their view, not away—to note cards, to even just one or two words scribbled in the order of worship. One of my favorites was a woman who turned a piece of typing paper sideways, drew a picture of the biblical scene and jotted words in bubbles around the edges. Given the diversity of possibilities in the middle ground, the key is to experiment. God knows we certainly have enough Sundays coming up to do that.

Personal Reflection

Has your system of notes changed from when you started preaching? How so? Is there a certain middle-ground approach that appeals to you? In an ideal world, how would you preach in relation to notes? Some? None? Middle ground?

Scriptural Meditation

"Lift up your hands to the holy place, and bless the LORD.*" (Psalm 134:2)*

More than Mechanics

When my student went blank in the middle of his sermon, it was an embarrassing moment for all of us. He was broken; that's the best word to describe it. Not only was he ashamed in front of his professor and peers, but he'd invited his wife to class that evening. When after the sermon and class discussion it came time to visit with him one on one, I invited his wife to join us, if they agreed. This excruciating moment became holy between the three of us; clearly Another was present.

They shared some personal struggles he had been experiencing, things I had not been aware of. There were tears. And great insight. We reflected together on how sermons are more than just words on a page or words in our mouths. Our hearts are present, too.

That night reminded me of a radical change I made in my teaching of preaching many years ago. It will sound crass—and maybe it was—but the way I used to teach the second course could best be described as a "baptized speech class." We paid attention to gestures, eye contact, posture, vocal projection, and so forth. A preaching lab. Those things are important, no doubt about it; but preaching is so much more than giving a speech. We give our hearts as well.

So whereas I used to suggest preachers work on gestures or eye contact, I suddenly realized that maybe the reason they had not made good eye contact had more to do with self-doubt than mechanics. You can tell somebody to look at the congregation, but, truth be told, if the sermon is not yet "ready for prime time," those self-doubts will often show through in our bodies: *Who am I to be telling these people about God?* Or perhaps the struggle is larger than this week's wrestling match with the text. Maybe the preacher is battling demons of depression, or addiction, or abuse. The list is legion. Advice to use more gestures would be like treating cancer with aspirin. The giving of sermons is not only a homiletical task but theological, biblical, pastoral, ethical, and, above all, personal. According to Frederick Buechner, it was Red Smith who claimed that being a writer is easy: just sit down at your desk and "open a vein."[28] It may not be a pretty picture—blood-letting and all—but something deeply personal happens when we preach.

Personal Reflection

What is the most embarrassing thing that has happened to you while preaching? How did you deal with it in the days that followed? What does it say to you now? In what ways do you feel present when you preach? In what ways do you feel absent? How does it feel to call yourself a preacher?

Scriptural Meditation

"You have made them a little lower than God, and crowned them with glory and honor." (Psalm 8:5)

Renewal
The Sacrament of Dessert

"Stressed spelled backwards is desserts. Coincidence? I think not."
—Anonymous

"Cookies are made of butter and love."
—Norwegian Proverb

It was most definitely an entrepreneur who came up with the idea of the dessert tray. How many times has my "No, thanks, I'm full" been vetoed by a piece of cheesecake looking at me from one of those trays? "On second thought, I guess I do have room for a little dessert. Anybody want to split something?" Yes, I know all about calories and the harmful effects of too much sugar in the diet; but as Robert Farrar Capon says of a fellow he knew who was counting calories, "His body may or may not lose weight; his soul, however, is sure to wither."[29]

I remember one time preaching at a church whose minister had a small chalkboard on her door for leaving messages. At the top it said: "Things to Do." One of the youth had written, "Eat cake." Not bad advice. When our kids were younger, we used to love reading Patricia Polacco's *Thunder Cake*. It's the story of how a wise grandmother teaches her granddaughter not to fear thunderstorms. I won't spoil it for you, but part of the process involves baking a cake, the recipe for which is included in the book. What great fun!

In that same spirit, one of our family's favorites is affectionately known as Nanny Nut Bars, named after my wife's late grandmother, who went by the nickname Nanny. Here's the recipe:

3/4 cup oil	1 egg
1 cup sugar	1 cup chopped pecans
1/4 cup honey	2 cups flour
1/2 teaspoon salt	1 teaspoon cinnamon
1 teaspoon vanilla	1 teaspoon baking soda

Mix ingredients together in large bowl until thoroughly moist. Spread in 9 x 11 glass pan and bake at 350° for approximately 25 minutes or until the center is no longer gooey. Let cool and cut into squares. You'll know what to do after that.

Preacher Dates

— Bake several of your favorite sweets and share them with friends
— Eat a light dinner and then treat yourself to one of those "all you can eat" dessert bars
— Take a cooking course on dessert making
— Savor a piece of chocolate as slowly as you can
— Buy a copy of Polacco's *Thunder Cake* and enjoy the treat
— Enter a cake baking contest; better yet, volunteer to judge one

"Research tells us fourteen out of any ten individuals like chocolate."
—Sandra Boynton

"Forget love. I'd rather fall in chocolate."
—Anonymous

Concluding Matters

SEVEN

PREACHING WITH JOY

We began our journey with a question—if preaching is intended to enliven the church, why is it killing so many ministers?—and moved quickly to the part about its killing us. But what about the first part, the line about enlivening the congregation? What of the power of God to bring about new life through preaching?

In the spring of 2005 I was invited back to Princeton Theological Seminary, where I had first presented the material for this book in the summer of 2004. I spent one free evening in a coffee shop across the street from the university, sipping on a hot chocolate and reading Anne Lamott's then new book, *Plan B*. One story in it I found especially intriguing, the story of a Hasidic rabbi who taught his students that if they studied the Torah, it would put Scripture on their hearts. When asked, Why *on* our hearts, and not *in* their hearts? the rabbi replied, "Only God can put Scripture inside. But reading sacred text can put it on your hearts, and then when your hearts break, the holy words will fall inside."[1]

I closed the book for a moment and thought about that image before picking up a copy of the *New York Times*. There on the front page was that awful story of Chicago judge Joan Humphrey Lefkow, living under federal protection after her husband and mother were murdered in their Chicago home. Police suspected it was likely the result of a ruling she had made on the bench. It was the kind of story that rips your heart out. She wondered how she would go on, how she would raise four daughters by herself now. The *Times* had pictures of the family before the murders. Near the end of the story came this one sentence, an absolutely amazing sentence: "She said she was taking comfort in a sermon about brokenness she heard years ago at St. Luke's Episcopal Church in Evanston, where her daughters sang in the choir and she makes sandwiches for the homeless once a month."[2]

This poor woman's heart had broken, and now, drawing on a sermon she'd heard years ago, the word of God was getting inside her heart. I knew then that I would share that word with those pastors gathered at Princeton. That story reminded me again of preaching's ability to enliven people, including preachers. Even when we have grown disheartened, we ourselves are renewed when we recall that preaching really does renew us—not just parishioners but preachers too. While we strive to create sermons that will renew the congregation, God is always at work in us preachers, offering personal renewal.

If you look in the dictionary, next to a certain entry, you'll often find a picture. Consider some playful examples. Like if you look under *wind*, imagine finding a picture of Chicago. Or if you look under *golf*, imagine finding a picture of Tiger Woods. That sort of thing. For some time now, I have wished that if you looked in the dictionary under joy, you would find a picture of a preacher. Oh, there would be other pictures. Boston Red Sox fans after the 2004 World Series, for instance. Or maybe that's the picture beside *euphoric*. Still, I long to see more joyful preachers.

I know some ministers who love preaching. Are there weeks when their love is not so romantic and the task is overwhelming? Absolutely, but still they love the call of God on their lives to preach the word. Another word in the dictionary comes to mind: *amateur*, which you may recall means "for the love of something," as opposed to a professional, who works for pay. I look forward to payday as much as the next person—some months more than others—but I would preach for nothing. Wouldn't you?

Before the International Olympic Committee permitted athletes to compete as professionals, the games were for amateurs, men and women who loved their sport. Period. The women's figure-skating finals for the 2002 winter games in Salt Lake City recaptured some of that innocence and joy and love. I don't know if you watched or, if you did, whether you remember the events that transpired. I was so moved I ordered a copy of the video and now show it to ministers in retreat settings. As I set up the scene for us to watch it, they're never quite sure what this has to do with preaching. "Just watch," I tell them. "You might be surprised."

Michelle Kwan, representing the United States, was supposed to win. Her challengers were formidable and from all over the world. And then there was the unknown American skater, Sarah Hughes, sixteen-year-old Sarah Hughes. She wasn't even expected to place, but what did she care? She was sixteen. She was there to skate, enjoy this great moment, and perhaps be back in four years to skate for the gold. The pressure was on Kwan and her challengers.

After the compulsories the previous night, somehow Hughes was in fourth place. She took to the ice, nervous I'm sure, but for those few minutes she skated the way only a sixteen-year-old can, someone who simply loves to skate. I can't do it justice, but I'll try. She starts off well enough, nailing her first jump, and you can tell she's pleased. As she continues, she nails every jump. You can feel the excitement in the announcers' voices. At one point they tell us she probably wouldn't even need to try another triple twisting move, but she does. Over and over, she keeps nailing jump after jump—axles and triple-toe loops and lutzes and twists and sow cows, who of us can tell the difference. When finally she finishes spiraling and the music stops, you can almost see her lips mouth these words, "Oh, my God!" Exactly.

When the clip is over, I stop the machine and turn off the television set. I turn the lights back on with tears in my eyes. I've seen it several times, and I still get emotional every time. And so do many of the preachers in the room. Sarah Hughes's movements on ice are beautiful, her expressions priceless. When finally I find the words to speak, this is what I say, "Joy. She skated for joy. That's the way we're intended to preach, for joy!"

Four little words: "I can still preach!" Those words from the mouth of a pastor in Texas, words that touched the life of her seminary professor, and later my life, and eventually the life of a Presbyterian pastor in Missouri. Four little words: "I can still preach!" I hope you feel that way. As Ronald Rolheiser notes, "The best way to thank a gift giver is to thoroughly enjoy the gift."[3] Or to paraphrase Irenaeus, the glory of God is a preacher who is fully alive.

Scriptural Meditation

"*Have mercy on me, O God, according to your steadfast love.*" (*Psalm 51:1*)

NOTES

Chapter 1   An Invitation to the Reader

1. David Steindl-Rast, *Gratefulness: The Heart of Prayer* (New York: Paulist Press, 1984), v.

2. There are some titles, old and new, that do acknowledge the more personal aspects of the preaching task. For instance, see Linda L. Clader, *Voicing the Vision: Imagination and Prophetic Preaching* (Harrisburg, PA: Morehouse Publishing, 2003); Robert C. Dykstra, *Discovering a Sermon: Personal Pastoral Preaching* (St. Louis: Chalice Press, 2001); David J. Schlafer, *Your Way with God's Word* (Cambridge, MA: Cowley Publications, 1995); Barbara Brown Taylor, *The Preaching Life* (Cambridge, MA: Cowley Publications, 1993); and Richard F. Ward, *Speaking from the Heart: Preaching with Passion* (Nashville: Abingdon Press, 1992).

3. For example, see Charles L. Campbell, *Preaching Jesus: New Directions for Homiletics in Hans Frei's Postliberal Theology* (Grand Rapids: Wm. B. Eerdmans Publishing Co., 1997); David J. Lose, *Confessing Jesus Christ: Preaching in a Postmodern World* (Grand Rapids: Wm. B. Eerdmans Publishing Co., 2003); and André Resner Jr., *Preacher and Cross: Person and Message in Theology and Rhetoric* (Grand Rapids: Wm. B. Eerdmans Publishing Co., 1999), all of which, interestingly enough, discuss the relation of theology and rhetoric for preaching.

4. William Wordsworth's expression "dull of soul" is cited in Esther de Waal, *Lost in Wonder: Rediscovering the Spiritual Art of Attentiveness* (Collegeville, MN: Liturgical Press, 2003), 2.

5. e. e. cummings, Introduction to his *Collected Poems* (New York: Harcourt, Brace & World, 1923), n.p.

6. Anne Lamott, *Bird by Bird: Some Instructions on Writing and Life* (New York: Anchor Books, 1994), 178.

7. Karl Barth, *Church Dogmatics*, III/4, *The Doctrine of Creation*, ed. G. W. Bromily and T. F. Torrance (Edinburgh: T. & T. Clark, 1969), 68, cited in Thomas W. Currie, "Jesus, Thou Joy of Loving Hearts," *Journal for Preachers* 29 (Lent 2006): 28.

8. Parker J. Palmer, *A Hidden Wholeness: The Journey toward an Undivided Life* (San Francisco: Jossey-Bass, 2004), 14–17.

9. O. Wesley Allen Jr., "Deeper Exegesis," unpublished papers of the 2004 Academy of Homiletics, 22.

10. Richard Lischer, *The End of Words: The Language of Reconciliation in a Culture of Violence* (Grand Rapids: Wm. B. Eerdmans Publishing Co., 2005), 76–81.

11. Richard J. Foster, *Celebration of Discipline: The Path to Spiritual Growth*, rev. ed. (San Francisco: Harper & Row, 1988). He names three categories of disciplines: inward, outward, and corporate. Even so, his outward category (simplicity, solitude, submission, and service) is grounded in a monastic approach.

12. The original quote by Irenaeus is found in his *Against Heresies*, IV.20.7. for a helpful discussion of Irenaeus's theology, see Jaroslav Pelikan, *The Christian Tradition: A History of the Development of Doctrine*, vol. 1, *The Emergence of the Catholic Tradition (100–600)* (Chicago: University of Chicago Press, 1971), 82–94. A fascinating discussion of docetism and preaching theory is found in Clyde E. Fant, *Preaching for Today*, rev. ed. (San Francisco: Harper & Row, 1987), 69–91. Special thanks to my colleague Robert Johnson for helpful insights into Irenaeus's historical context.

13. C. S. Lewis, *The Screwtape Letters* (New York: HarperCollins, 2003), 63–64, 66.

14. Nancy M. Malone, *Walking a Literary Labyrinth: A Spirituality of Reading* (New York: Riverhead Books, 2003), 179–80.

15. Julia Cameron, *The Sound of Paper: Starting from Scratch* (New York: Jeremy P. Tarcher/Penguin, 2004), 8.

16. R. E. C. Browne, *The Ministry of the Word* (London: SCM Press, 1958), 49–50. A more recent use of the bread metaphor is found in Clader, *Voicing the Vision*, 14–17.

17. Julia Cameron, *The Artist's Way: A Spiritual Path to Higher Creativity*, 10th anniv. ed. (New York: Jeremy P. Tarcher/Putnam, 2002), 19.

Chapter 2   Creating and Re-creating

1. Henry David Thoreau, "Life without Principle," in *The Portable Thoreau*, ed. Carl Bode (New York: Penguin Books, 1975), 636.

2. Linda Carolyn Loving, in *Birthing the Sermon: Women Preachers on the Creative Process*, ed. Jana Childers (St. Louis: Chalice Press, 2001), 101–2.

3. This image is adapted from the epilogue to David Gelernter's *Mirror Worlds: Or the Day Software Puts the Universe in a Shoebox: How It Will Happen and What It Will Mean* (New York: Oxford University Press, 1991), 221.

4. Parker J. Palmer, *The Active Life: A Spirituality of Work, Creativity, and Caring* (San Francisco: Jossey-Bass, 1990), 15–16. Much thanks to my colleague Molly Marshall for putting me on to this helpful source.

5. Palmer, *The Active Life*, 16.

6. Dorothy Bass, *Receiving the Day: Christian Practices for Opening the Gift of Time* (San Francisco: Jossey-Bass, 2000), 45.

7. Julia Cameron, *The Artist's Way: A Spiritual Path to Higher Creativity*, 10th anniv. ed. (New York: Jeremy P. Tarcher/Putnam, 2002), 98.

8. Julia Cameron, *The Sound of Paper: Starting from Scratch* (New York: Jeremy P. Tarcher/Penguin, 2004), 37.

9. Palmer, *The Active Life*, 15.

10. Parker J. Palmer, *A Hidden Wholeness: The Journey toward an Undivided Life* (San Francisco: Jossey-Bass, 2004), 46–47.

11. This story is retold in Ronald Rolheiser, *Against an Infinite Horizon: The Finger of God in Our Everyday Lives*, rev. ed. (New York: Crossroad Publishing Co., 2001), 228.

12. James D. Watson, *The Double Helix: A Personal Account of the Discovery of the Structure of DNA* (New York: Atheneum, 1968). Thanks to John Walker for this insight.

13. Eberhard Busch, *The Great Passion: An Introduction to Karl Barth's Theology*, trans. Geoffrey W. Bromiley (Grand Rapids: Wm. B. Eerdmans Publishing Co., 2004), 5, 50.

14. Cited in Nancy M. Malone, *Walking a Literary Labyrinth: A Spirituality of Reading* (New York: Riverhead Books, 2003), 91.

15. Frederic M. Hudson, *The Adult Years: Mastering the Art of Self-Renewal* (San Francisco: Jossey-Bass, 1991), 98. Thanks to my colleague James Hines for sharing this quote.

16. Thomas Merton, *Day of a Stranger*, in *A Thomas Merton Reader*, ed. P. McDonnell (New York: Image Books, 1974), 436.

17. David Steindl-Rast, *The Music of Silence*, cited in Frederic and Mary Ann Brussat, *Spiritual Literacy: Reading the Sacred in Everyday Life* (New York: Scribner, 1996), 29.

18. Palmer, *The Active Life*, 4.

19. Simon Tugwell, *The Way of the Preacher* (London: Darton, Longman & Todd, 1979), 10. Thanks to my UK colleague at Spurgeon's College, Peter Stevenson, for pointing this out.

20. Barbara K. Lundblad, in Childers, *Birthing the Sermon*, 120.

21. Philip Toynbee, *Part of a Journey: An Autobiographical Journal 1977–79* (London: Collins, Fount Paperback, 1981), cited in Esther de Waal, *Lost in Wonder: Rediscovering the Spiritual Art of Attentiveness* (Collegeville, MN: Liturgical Press, 2003), 62.

22. de Waal, *Lost in Wonder*, 9.

23. Annie Dillard, *A Pilgrim at Tinker Creek* (New York: Perennial Classics, 1998), 17.

24. de Waal, *Lost in Wonder*, 7.

25. Gelernter, *Mirror Worlds*, 223–24.

26. John Ruskin, *Modern Painters*, vol. 3, cited in Gelernter, *Mirror Worlds*, 223.

27. "The Eyes Have It," *60 Minutes*, broadcast on CBS, January 4, 2004.

28. Michael Goldman, cited in Dillard, *Pilgrim at Tinker Creek*, 85.

Chapter 3   Stage One: Studying the Scriptures

1. Marilynne Robinson, *Gilead* (New York: Farrar, Straus & Giroux, 2004), 232.

2. Linda Carolyn Loving, in *Birthing the Sermon: Women Preachers on the Creative Process*, ed. Jana Childers (St. Louis: Chalice Press, 2001), 102.

3. Ted Kooser, *The Poetry Home Repair Manual: Practical Advice for Beginning Poets* (Lincoln, NE: University of Nebraska Press, 2005), 12–13.

4. Cited in Kay Redfield Jamison, *Exuberance: The Passion for Life* (New York: Vintage Books, 2004), 217.

5. Julia Cameron, *The Right to Write: An Invitation and Initiation into the Writing Life* (New York: Jeremy P. Tarcher/Putnam, 1998), 89.

6. Rollo May, *The Courage to Create* (New York: W. W. Norton & Co., 1975), 27.

7. Cameron, *The Right to Write*, 223.

8. Ibid., 223.

9. Julia Cameron, *The Sound of Paper: Starting from Scratch* (New York: Jeremy P. Tarcher/Penguin, 2004), 106.

10. Fred B. Craddock, *Preaching* (Nashville: Abingdon Press, 1985), 84–85.

11. Jill Krementz, *The Writer's Desk* (New York: Random House, 1996), xii, 107. Thanks to graduate assistant Cynthia Jarrold for telling me about this source.

12. Rebecca Solnit, *Wanderlust: A History of Walking* (New York: Viking Penguin, 2000), 5.

13. Ibid., 10.

14. Cameron, *The Sound of Paper*, 116.

15. Ibid., 81–84.

16. Solnit, *Wanderlust*, 160.

17. Henry David Thoreau, "Walking," in *The Portable Thoreau*, ed. Carl Bode (New York: Penguin Books, 1975), 594.

18. Ibid., 592, 630.

19. Cited in Solnit, *Wanderlust*, 12–14.

20. Cited in Jamison, *Exuberance*, 21.

21. Cited in Krementz, *The Writer's Desk*, 37.

22. Cameron, *The Sound of Paper*, 128.

23. Kathleen Norris, *The Virgin of Bennington* (New York: Riverhead Books, 2001), 49.

24. Barry Schwartz, *The Paradox of Choice: Why More Is Less* (New York: HarperCollins, 2004), 77–78.

25. Mike Graves, "The Trouble with Jet Stream Preaching," *Preaching*, September–October 1990, 39–41.

26. Stephen Farris, "With the Aid of Spectacles: Teaching

Exegesis in Preaching Class," in the unpublished papers of the 2004 Academy of Homiletics, 9.

27. Cited in Walter C. Kaiser Jr., *Toward an Exegetical Theology: Biblical Exegesis for Preaching and Teaching* (Grand Rapids: Baker Book House, 1981), 200.

28. Barbara Holland, *Endangered Pleasures: In Defense of Naps, Bacon, Martinis, Profanity, and Other Indulgences* (New York: Perennial, 2000), 37.

29. Thierry Paquot, *The Art of the Siesta*, trans. Ken Hollings (London: Marion Boyars Publishers, 2003), 42.

30. Ibid., 8–9.

31. Cited in William A. Anthony, *The Art of Napping* (New York: Larson Publications, 1997), 10.

32. Eugene L. Lowry, *Living with the Lectionary: Preaching through the Revised Common Lectionary* (Nashville: Abingdon Press, 1992); and Shelley E. Cochran, *The Pastor's Underground Guide to the Revised Common Lectionary*, 3 vols. (St. Louis: Chalice Press, 1997).

33. David Buttrick, *Speaking Parables: A Homiletic Guide* (Louisville, KY: Westminster John Knox Press, 2000), xiv.

34. I recently ran across a version of this in Dwight E. Stevenson's *In the Biblical Preacher's Workshop* (Nashville: Abingdon Press, 1967), 81–82, although I think I first learned of it from one of my preaching professors, Al Fasol. For a different take on preparing three sermons in intervals, see O. Wesley Allen Jr., *The Homiletic of All Believers: A Conversational Approach* (Louisville, KY: Westminster John Knox Press, 2005), chapters 4 and 5. As for the chronology of my own chart, I am fully aware that the Lord's Day is the first day of the week, the first day of the new creation made possible in Christ's resurrection; I am also aware that for most of us ministers the week is leading up to Sundays.

35. Malcolm Gladwell, *The Tipping Point: How Little Things Can Make a Big Difference* (New York: Little, Brown & Co., 2000), 99, refers to a study by an advertising firm, "Whenever there are at least four different 15-second commercials in a two-and-a-half minute commercial time-out, the effectiveness of any one 15-second ad sinks to almost zero."

36. H. Grady Davis, *Design for Preaching* (Philadelphia: Fortress Press, 1958), 15.

37. Jana Childers, ed., *The Purposes of Preaching* (St. Louis: Chalice Press, 2004).

38. James A. Sanders, *God Has a Story Too: Sermons in Context* (Philadelphia: Fortress Press, 1979), 16–26.

39. Mike Graves, "God of Grace and Glory: The Focus of Our Preaching," in *What's the Matter with Preaching Today?* ed. Mike Graves (Louisville, KY: Westminster John Knox Press, 2004), 109–25.

Chapter 4   Stage Two: Brainstorming Stories

1. Another interesting debate in recent years is whether biblical preachers must always employ a text. See, for instance, David Buttrick, *A Captive Voice: The Liberation of Preaching* (Louisville, KY: Westminster John Knox Press, 1994); and Edward Farley, *Practicing Gospel: Unconventional Thoughts on the Church's Ministry* (Louisville, KY: Westminster John Knox Press, 2003), especially chapters 6 and 7.

2. While multiple volumes have been written by theologians and homileticians alike, for a succinct and helpful overview of the debate, see Thomas G. Long's essay, "And How Shall They Hear?: The Listener in Contemporary Preaching," in *Listening to the Word: Studies in Honor of Fred B. Craddock*, ed. Gail R. O'Day and Thomas G. Long (Nashville: Abingdon Press, 1993), 172–76. For a recent example of aversion to stories from outside the biblical materials, see Ellen F. Davis, *Wondrous Depth: Preaching the Old Testament* (Louisville, KY: Westminster John Knox Press, 2005), 129, who compares searching for interesting stories to the food industry's practice of adding nutritional additives to food stripped of its vitamins in processing. She adds, "The passage itself provides the story."

3. For instance, there is the story about the time Barth told an illustration based on the sinking of the *Titanic*, only to regret it later. Eugene L. Lowry, *The Sermon: Dancing the Edge of Mystery* (Nashville: Abingdon Press, 1997), 30.

4. While many homiletics texts devote a few pages to the subject, Richard L. Thulin has written an entire monograph on autobiography in his volume *The "I" of the Sermon: Autobiography in the Pulpit* (Minneapolis: Fortress Press, 1989).

5. David Buttrick, *Homiletic: Moves and Structures* (Philadelphia: Fortress Press, 1987), 141–43, emphasis Buttrick's.

6. While Craddock has on occasion referred to his use of self-disclosure as probably more than is recommended in sound homiletical theory (workshop at the General Assembly of the Christian Church, Disciples of Christ, in Denver, Colorado, July 25–29, 1997), Joseph M. Webb, *Comedy and Preaching* (St. Louis: Chalice Press, 1998), 61–63, is probably more accurate when he describes Craddock as the "off-camera voice" in his stories.

7. Thomas G. Long, *The Witness of Preaching*, 2nd ed. (Louisville, KY: Westminster John Knox Press, 2005), 221.

8. A. A. Milne, cited in Calvin Miller, *Spirit, Word, and Story: A Philosophy of Preaching* (Dallas: Word Publishing, 1989), 140.

9. Long, *The Witness of Preaching*, 2nd ed., 221.

10. Ibid., 204–18. I have adapted two of these types from Long, who in his second edition has renamed the three types of illustrations: the analogy, the example, and the metaphor.

11. Andy Crouch, "We're Rich," in *The Best Christian Writing 2004*, ed. John Wilson (San Francisco: Jossey-Bass, 2004), 29.

12. See the excellent critique and alternative suggestions in Sara Covin Juengst, *Sharing Faith with Children: Rethinking the Children's Sermon* (Louisville, KY: Westminster John Knox Press, 1994).

13. Adapted from Fred B. Craddock, *Craddock Stories*, ed. Mike Graves and Richard F. Ward (St. Louis: Chalice Press, 2001), 118.

14. Frederick Buechner, *Whistling in the Dark: A Doubter's Dictionary* (San Francisco: HarperSanFrancisco, 1993), 93–94.

15. Richard Lischer, *Open Secrets: A Spiritual Journey through a Country Church* (New York: Doubleday, 2001), 9–10.

16. Gail Ramshaw, *Treasures Old and New: Images in the Lectionary* (Minneapolis: Fortress Press, 2002).

17. Julia Cameron, *The Artist's Way: A Spiritual Path to Higher Creativity*, 10th anniv. ed. (New York: Jeremy P. Tarcher/Putnam, 2002), 7.

18. Cited in Simon Tugwell, *The Way of the Preacher* (London: Darton, Longman & Todd, 1979), 26.

19. Julia Cameron, *The Sound of Paper: Starting from Scratch* (New York: Jeremy P. Tarcher/Penguin 2004), 98.

20. Anne Lamott, *Bird by Bird: Some Instructions on Writing and Life* (New York: Anchor Books, 1994), 178.

21. Nancy M. Malone, *Walking a Literary Labyrinth: A Spirituality of Reading* (New York: Riverhead Books, 2003), 54.

22. Annie Dillard, *The Writing Life* (New York: HarperPerennial, 1989), 72.

23. Jackson W. Carroll, "Pastor's Picks: What Preachers Are Reading," *The Christian Century*, August 23, 2003, 31–33.

24. Sara Nelson, *So Many Books, So Little Time: A Year of Passionate Reading* (New York: G. P. Putnam's Sons, 2003).

25. Annie Dillard, "A Girl and Her Books," *American Educator* (Fall 1989):42.

26. Cited in Alberto Manguel, *A History of Reading* (New York: Viking, 1996), 1.

27. Malone, *Walking a Literary Labyrinth*, 19.

28. David Steindl-Rast, *Gratefulness: The Heart of Prayer* (New York: Paulist Press, 1984), 40, cited in Don E. Saliers, *Worship as Theology: Foretaste of Glory Divine* (Nashville: Abingdon Press, 1994), 87.

29. Azar Nafisi, *Reading Lolita in Tehran: A Memoir in Books* (New York: Random House, 2004), 111.

30. Cited in Cameron, *The Sound of Paper*, 117.

31. Elizabeth Barrett Browning, "Aurora Leigh," in *The Poetical Works of Elizabeth Barrett Browning* (New York: Macmillan, 1897), 466.

32. Mary Oliver, "Low Tide," *Amicus Journal* (Winter 2001): 34, cited in Parker J. Palmer, *A Hidden Wholeness: The Journey toward an Undivided Life* (San Francisco: Jossey-Bass, 2004), 34.

33. Frederic and Mary Ann Brussat, *Spiritual Literacy: Reading the Sacred in Everyday Life* (New York: Scribner, 1996).

34. Ibid., 15.

35. Cited in Jill Krementz, *The Writer's Desk* (New York: Random House, 1996), 17.

36. Don Wardlaw adapted this idea from Dwight E. Stevenson, *In the Biblical Preacher's Workshop* (Nashville: Abingdon Press, 1967), 75–80. Thanks to Richard Ward for reminding me of Wardlaw's "gremlins."

37. Malone, *Walking a Literary Labyrinth*, 152.

38. Henri J. M. Nouwen, *Sabbatical Journey: The Diary of His Final Year* (New York: Crossroad Publishing Co., 1998), 7.

Chapter 5   Stage Three: Creating a Sequence

1. John Ciardi, *Dialogue with an Audience* (Philadelphia: Lippincott, 1963), 19–20, cited in William E. Hull, "The Poetry of God," *The Christian Ministry*, May 1985, 26.

2. H. W. Janson, *History of Art*, 4th ed., rev. and expanded by Anthony F. Janson (New York: Harry N. Abrams, 1991), 44–47.

3. Dorothy Sayers, *The Mind of the Maker* (New York: Harper & Brothers, 1941), 22.

4. See André Resner Jr., *Preacher and Cross* (Grand Rapids: Wm. B. Eerdmans Publishing Co., 1999), 42–44, who tells of Jerome's bizarre obsession with repenting of things rhetorical.

5. Augustine, *On Christian Teaching*, Book IV.4, trans. and with an intro. by R. P. H. Green (Oxford: Oxford University Press, 1997), 101.

6. For instance, see Lucy Lind Hogan and Robert Reid, *Connecting with the Congregation: Rhetoric and the Art of Preaching* (Nashville: Abingdon Press, 1999); and James F. Kay, "Reorientation: Homiletics and Theologically Authorized Rhetoric," *Princeton Seminary Bulletin* 24 (2003):16–35.

7. Cicero's five canons include invention (deciding what to say), arrangement (deciding how to say it and in what order), style (the language to be used), memory (committing to memory), and delivery (presenting the material).

8. Martin Marty, "Interestingness and Imagination," *Word and World* 5 (Summer 1985):236–37.

9. Eugene L. Lowry, *The Homiletical Plot: The Sermon as Narrative Art Form*, expanded ed. (Louisville, KY: Westminster John Knox Press, 2001), 59–60.

10. Cited in Jill Krementz, *The Writer's Desk* (New York: Random House, 1996), 10.

11. David McCullough, *Truman* (New York: Touchstone, 1992), 984, cited in Thomas G. Long, *Testimony: Talking Ourselves into Being Christian* (San Francisco: Jossey-Bass, 2004), 60.

12. Michael Gelb, *How to Think like Leonardo da Vinci: Seven Steps to Genius Everyday* (New York: Dell, 1998), 158, cited in Jim Loehr and Tony Schwartz, *The Power of Full Engagement* (New York: Free Press, 2003), 96.

13. G. K. Chesterton, cited in Frederick Buechner, *Speak What*

We Feel (Not What We Ought to Say): Reflections on Literature and Faith (San Francisco: HarperSanFrancisco, 2001), 119.

14. Mary Cartledgehayes, *Grace: A Memoir* (New York: Crown Publishers, 2003), 293.

15. Cited in J. Scott, "When Child's Play Is Too Simple," *New York Times*, July 15, 2000.

16. Fred B. Craddock, *As One without Authority* (Nashville: Abingdon Press, 1971). This important work has been revised and reissued by Chalice Press (2001).

17. Cleophus J. LaRue, "Two Ships Passing in the Night," in *What's the Matter with Preaching Today?* ed. Mike Graves (Louisville, KY: Westminster John Knox Press, 2004), 127–44.

18. C. H. Dodd, *The Parables of the Kingdom*, rev. ed. (New York: Charles Scribner's Sons, 1961), 5.

19. For instance, see Craddock, *As One without Authority*, rev. ed., 37–38; 45.

20. Ibid., 46.

21. Eugene L. Lowry, *The Homiletical Plot* (Atlanta: John Knox Press, 1980).

22. Ibid., 22–26.

23. See Eugene L. Lowry, *How to Preach a Parable: Designs for Narrative Sermons* (Nashville: Abingdon Press, 1989), 38–40, who discusses four design strategies.

24. Christopher C. Rowland, "Introduction," in his commentary on Revelation in *New Interpreter's Bible*, vol. 12 (Nashville: Abingdon Press, 1998), 507.

25. Lowry, *How to Preach a Parable*, 73. Lowry prefers to discuss a continuum called "Distance between Teller and Story," in which he cautions against too much direct discourse, during which listeners might be tempted to gauge our acting abilities or too much preacher voice, whereby the narrative degenerates into exposition.

26. Interview with Fred B. Craddock, September 13, 1999, Cherry Log, Georgia. See also Eugene L. Lowry, "The Revolution of Sermonic Shape," in *Listening to the Word: Studies in Honor of Fred B. Craddock*, ed. Gail R. O'Day and Thomas G. Long (Nashville: Abingdon Press, 1993), 99. Thomas G. Long, "Form," in *Concise Encyclopedia of Preaching*, ed. William H. Willimon and Richard

Lischer (Louisville, KY: Westminster John Knox Press, 1995), 150, discusses narrative and inductive as "aspects of a more general approach to sermon structure."

27. David Buttrick, *Homiletic: Moves and Structures* (Philadelphia: Fortress Press, 1987), 23–28.

28. Barry Schwartz, *The Paradox of Choice: Why More Is Less* (New York: HarperCollins, 2004), 49.

29. Ted Kooser, *The Poetry Home Repair Manual: Practical Advice for Beginning Poets* (Lincoln, NE: University of Nebraska Press, 2005), 30.

30. Thomas Lynch, "Reno," in his collection of essays, *Bodies in Motion and at Rest: On Metaphor and Mortality* (New York: W. W. Norton & Co., 2000), 256.

31. Stephen Nachmanovitch, *Free Play: Improvisation in Life and Art* (Los Angeles: Jeremy P. Tarcher, 1990), .

32. Robert C. Dykstra, *Discovering a Sermon: Personal Pastoral Preaching* (St. Louis: Chalice Press, 2001), 11–12.

33. Carl Honoré, *In Praise of Slowness: Challenging the Cult of Speed* (New York: HarperCollins, 2004), 120.

34. Kooser, *The Poetry Home Repair Manual*, 17.

35. Julia Cameron, *The Artist's Way: A Spiritual Path to Higher Creativity*, 10th anniv. ed. (New York: Jeremy P. Tarcher/Putnam, 2002), 195.

36. Noah Adams, *Piano Lessons: Music, Love, and True Adventures* (New York: Delta, 1997), 109.

Chapter 6   Stage Four: Embodying the Sermon

1. See Richard F. Ward, *Speaking from the Heart: Preaching with Passion* (Nashville: Abingdon Press, 1992), and Jana Childers, *Performing the Word: Preaching as Theatre* (Nashville: Abingdon Press, 1998).

2. See Jana Childers, ed., *Birthing the Sermon: Women Preachers on the Creative Process* (St. Louis: Chalice Press, 2001).

3. Julia Cameron, *The Right to Write: An Invitation and Initiation into the Writing Life* (New York: Jeremy P. Tarcher/Putnam, 1998), 62.

4. Anne Lamott, *Plan B: Further Thoughts on Faith* (New York: Riverhead Books, 2005), 106–8.

5. Don M. Wardlaw, *Preaching Preference Profile*, videotape (n.p.: Takestock Ministries, 1988).

6. Malcom Gladwell, *Blink: The Power of Thinking without Thinking* (New York: Little, Brown & Co., 2005), 12–13, shows how students' snap judgments based on watching ten-second video clips of teachers are essentially the same after a full semester in the classroom with those teachers.

7. Ron Hoff, *I Can See You Naked: A Fearless Guide to Making Great Presentations* (Kansas City, MO: Andrews McMeel Publishing, 1988).

8. Doris Lessing, cited in Julia Cameron, *The Artist's Way: A Spiritual Path to Higher Creativity*, 10th anniv. ed. (New York: Jeremy P. Tarcher/Putnam, 2002), 42.

9. Jim Loehr and Tony Schwartz, *The Power of Full Engagement* (New York: Free Press, 2003), 4–9.

10. David Steindl-Rast, *Gratefulness: The Heart of Prayer* (New York: Paulist Press, 1984), 75.

11. Cited in Kay Redfield Jamison, *Exuberance: The Passion for Life* (New York: Vintage Books, 2004), 83.

12. Mary Cartledgehayes, *Grace: A Memoir* (New York: Crown Publishers, 2003), 59.

13. Marilynne Robinson, *Gilead* (New York: Farrar, Straus & Giroux, 2004), 18, 40, 245.

14. See Ward, *Speaking from the Heart,* esp. chapters 3 and 4.

15. Frederick Buechner, *Telling Secrets* (San Francisco: HarperSanFrancisco, 1991), 61.

16. Thomas Merton, *The Sign of Jonas* (London: Hollis & Carter, 1953), 56–57, cited in Richard B. Hays, " 'Writing for God After All'—Scripture, Poetry, and Proclamation," *Theological Education* 31 (1994):113.

17. Stanley P. Saunders and Charles L. Campbell, *The Word on the Street: Performing the Scriptures in the Urban Context* (Grand Rapids: Wm. B. Eerdmans Publishing Co., 2000), 96. The student's reaction encompasses more than preaching without notes, but that was part of her journey.

18. Joseph M. Webb, *Preaching without Notes* (Nashville: Abingdon Press, 2001), 35–36.

19. See Fred B. Craddock, *As One without Authority*, rev. ed. (St. Louis: Chalice Press, 2001), 45–47, who claims that in traditional models of preaching, the move from point I, subpoint 2 back to point II, subpoint 1 is rarely logical.

20. Cited in Jamison, *Exuberance*, 92.

21. Cited in Tom Harpur, *The Spirituality of Wine* (Kelowna, BC, Canada: Northstone Publishing, 2004), 154.

22. Thomas C. Foster, *How to Read Literature like a Professor* (New York: Quill, 2003), 8.

23. Alexander Schmemann, *For the Life of the World*, rev. ed. (Crestwood, NY: St. Vladimir's Seminary Press, 2002), 16.

24. Bobi Jones, "Having Our Tea," in *The Lion Christian Poetry Collection*, comp. Mary Batchelor (Oxford: Lion Publishing, 1995), 343.

25. Sara Covin Juengst, *Breaking Bread: The Spiritual Significance of Food* (Louisville, KY: Westminster/John Knox Press, 1992), 16.

26. Edgar Watson Howe, cited in Sara Covin Juengst, *Sharing Faith with Children: Rethinking the Children's Sermon* (Louisville, KY: Westminster John Knox Press, 1994), 15.

27. Robert Farrar Capon, *The Supper of the Lamb: A Culinary Reflection* (New York: Random House, 2002), 40.

28. Frederick Buechner, *Speak What We Feel (Not What We Ought to Say): Reflections on Literature and Faith* (San Francisco: HarperSanFrancisco, 2001), ix.

29. Capon, *The Supper of the Lamb*, 112.

Chapter 7   Preaching with Joy

1. Anne Lamott, *Plan B: Further Thoughts on Faith* (New York: Riverhead Books, 2005), 73.

2. *New York Times*, March 10, 2005, sec. A, 1, 22.

3. Ronald Rolheiser, *Against an Infinite Horizon: The Finger of God in Our Everyday Lives*, rev. ed. (New York: Crossroad Publishing Co., 2001), 80.